FOR GOD'S SAKE

Jonathan Blake has worked ~~with~~ ~~the Missionaries~~ of Charity in Calcutta; been a ~~priest in~~ ~~the~~ Church of England; qualified as a financial adviser; served as the international youth co-ordinator and the UK's co-secretary general of the World Conference on Religion and Peace and directed the Week of Prayer for World Peace, both of them international and interfaith organisations; he has also been a Samaritan and a marriage guidance counsellor.

As a minister working independently of any denomination since 1994, he has conducted services in the UK and abroad, in homes, gardens, churches, hotels, country estates, pubs, clubs, cruisers, castles, marquees and a circus ring, as well as on top of Snowdon, under water and over the Internet.

Now living in Gillingham, Kent, he offers to conduct baptisms, naming and blessings, wedding ceremonies, funerals and all the usual and special liturgies, giving complete choice about venue, style and content to those involved, whatever their beliefs or philosophy. He also offers a consultancy service to clergy and to those in situations of personal conflict, as well as chairing the charity, The Holy Circle Trust.

FOR GOD'S SAKE
DON'T GO TO CHURCH

REVD JONATHAN BLAKE

ARTHUR JAMES
NEW ALRESFORD

First published in 1999 by

ARTHUR JAMES LTD
An imprint of John Hunt Publishing
46a West Street
New Alresford
Hampshire
SO24 9AU

A catalogue record for this book is available
from the British Library.

ISBN 0 85305 446 0

Typeset in 10/13 ITC Quorum Book
by Watermark, Cromer NR27 9HL

Printed in Great Britain by
Biddles Ltd, Guildford and King's Lynn

FOR MY BELOVED CHILDREN

HEIDI

AND JAMIESON

FOR EVER

MY MOST CHERISHED AND TREASURED

CONTENTS

*course — What would you like me to wear? — Other faiths, no
faith*

*The first UK wedding over the Internet — The wettest wedding —
The apple orchard — The castle ruins — The freedom to be — From
milking sheds to country barns — A London park — A selection of
foreign jaunts — Touching venues — Surprise, surprise! — Making
the ordinary extraordinary*

*You can't . . . — The true community — The tutting church —
Secretive and saucy churchwardens — It's about time — Always
bin a generalisation — Sex as a window to God — Over the edge —
Within the widest boundaries*

*Alternatives — Horror stories — The essentials in tragedy — The
funeral — And just a sprinkling of religio-speak — An art form —
You can't do that! — Skin deep reactions*

*The dreaded committee — Timid and trapped — But ministry to
pets, that's going too far! — Communion — Counselling — The
demon factor — And so much more — But would you do anything?*

*The cosy package — Information and choice — But who is your
boss? — Are you starting a cult? — But you are not encouraging
people to go to church! — Providing what's true*

PART ONE
DANGER!

1 GOVERNMENT HEALTH WARNING

Your local church is dangerous. In fact anything to do with religion generally is so hazardous it should carry a Government Health Warning!

People read all about the dangers of cults and feel superior because they believe they wouldn't be so foolish as to become involved in one.

However, the quaint parish church at the top of the road or the free church around the corner is every bit as dangerous. They are able to pretend to be respectable, hiding behind history and tradition, when in fact they often operate as cults and can severely damage those who become involved.

For some strange reason people are naïve when it comes to matters of faith. Even professional, well educated people appear to crumble when faced with the mysterious power of religion.

The church uses that power to trap and hurt the lives of ordinary people. This book is written to provide a warning and to offer advice about how people should protect themselves.

BE PREPARED!

Reading through these pages will be no easy ride. I have written in a deliberately punchy style and some readers, particularly if they come from a religious tradition, may be offended and want to put the book down. Please persevere.

Part One is a fairly savage critique of the church but Part Two offers a fresh and intriguing approach to the Christian faith. Part Three is my personal story, which will help you understand something of my experience. Part Four describes my new work and the extraordinary possibilities it creates.

You may prefer to read Part Three first if you want to know more about my life first. Certainly do that if you get bogged down in Part One, but I hope that if the book is read through as a whole it will inspire and empower those who are not involved in a church while also opening up creative and visionary thinking for church members.

LAMBS TO THE SLAUGHTER

On television and radio, religion pops up all over the place. Of course it is carefully vetted and so what we see and hear is largely sweet and innocuous. All the more deadly, for it lulls us into a false sense of security.

Our contact with the church starts so innocently. It may be as a youngster at youth club, a couple hoping for marriage, new parents planning a baptism, children joining Sunday school or mourners from a funeral.

Instantly the church has an advantage. It is able to gain access to our life at a moment of vulnerability and personal growth or change. The priest is able to ask searching questions, gain considerable information and choose to use that in whatever way he or she chooses.

Then comes the moment of judgment. Priests are allowed to play God in deciding how they will respond to our situations. If we say the right things and conform to the priest's expectations, it may be that we pass the test, all is well and we go away satisfied customers.

However, there are increasing numbers of very bruised people who even at this first stage are rejected. The priest won't marry them because they have been divorced, or they live together, or they already have a baby. The priest won't baptise their baby because they don't attend church or they don't like the idea of attending a six-week training course, or they were hoping for the service on a Sunday afternoon.

Each priest responds differently because it is left to him or her to decide. They have the power to say yes or no, the power to show mercy or to judge. As throughout history, those given such absolute power within an institution so often end up by abusing it in the name of God.

What you need to understand to stay safe is that there is a game being played by the priest and by the church in all these and other contacts — what we might call the hidden agenda.

THE HIDDEN AGENDA

What is not at first apparent to the newcomer is that behind the façade of kindness and care there lies an aim which the priest or church member is often ruthless in trying to achieve.

They want you to become a committed Christian, which to their way of thinking means joining their church. They want your bum on their pew or seat. They want your face in church on a Sunday. They want your money in the bag. They want you.

Once you realise this, it is easier to see through and protect yourself from much of what happens in a church. It is also tragic. Behind the smiles and laughter, the acts of kindness, the friendly conversations and mugs of coffee, there is this one aim buzzing in the air — to ensnare you.

ON THE SLIPPERY SLOPE

In fact if you analyse what happens in most churches, everything is geared to swelling numbers. Outside the building, bright, often humorous, posters promise a warm welcome to newcomers with bargains thrown in from God, like greater peace and deeper joy. Inside, trained members greet you as warmly as a lost friend and guide you to your seat. If the church is advanced, a 'be-friender' may come and sit with you. Afterwards coffee and biscuits are supplied, your name and address are taken and you are introduced to other members.

In the weeks that follow the priest may call, church members may visit, flowers might arrive, invitations may be received to parties, coffee mornings or other approp- riate groups. If you speak about problems or difficulties there are kind listening ears and helpful hands. Practical and personal care is plentiful.

If you are unaware of what's going on, it can come as a delightful surprise. Perhaps for the first time in ages you feel as though someone cares about you. You feel you belong. As though you've discovered a large family whose arms are open wide for you.

It can melt your heart and erode your carefully placed defences. You begin to assume that these are people you can trust with your life.

GOD IS THE ICING ON THE CAKE

Into this warm and intoxicating experience comes talk of God. The priest and church members suggest that it is all part and parcel of the whole package. Their warmth and care, the sense of family and belonging, comes from God.

What you don't know is that a carefully planned strategy is being followed. Individuals and prayer groups around the church have been fed your name as an item for earnest prayer. Every time you show a greater interest or ask a searching question, news flies through the church and the fire of prayer is stoked up further. They are after your soul!

It is so easy for you to be duped. You believe it is all genuine and you warm to the interest being shown to you. You begin to feel as though you belong, as though you have 'come home'. Into your cold world of struggle and difficulty has come something which speaks of problems solved, pain healed, questions answered. You are promised a pathway to follow with clear signposts – and a new family to travel with you. It's a 'Journey into Life' as one simplistic Christian book describes it.

You become entranced – one could almost say bewitched – and you find yourself asking, 'How do I become a committed Christian?'

IT'S JUST LIKE FALLING IN LOVE

The church member is quick to provide the answer. It all sounds so romantic. Jesus loves you and he wants you to love him too. He wants to become one with you and you with him. He wants your heart and your soul and your life, nothing less. If you give it to him then he'll move in. Lock, stock and barrel he'll set up home inside you. You'll never need to be alone again.

If you've been sucked in at this stage then there's not much hope, I'm afraid. Just like the star struck Romeo or the dewy eyed Juliet, you're a lost cause.

The experience of those who become 'committed Christians' is in fact almost exactly a reflection of what happens to them when they fall in love. Some go completely doolally, others manage it in an ordered and controlled way. Whichever way, the outcome is the same. You're well and truly hooked.

At this stage you have passed beyond reason, logic or common sense. Every part of you has been put into the service of Jesus. Your emotions and your intellect will only parrot Jesus.

Having to listen to a new convert is about as embarrassing as listening to a lovestruck teenager. I've been saved ... Jesus has found me ... he speaks to me every day ... I tell him everything ... his love is so wonderful ... I'd do anything for him. ...

Please don't dismiss this as the sort of extreme happenings in a cult. Oh no, this is bread and butter Christian ministry throughout this country in your local church. Of course the language and the style may be different. No two romances are the same, but the intention and the hidden agenda are largely the same.

EASY PREY

Of course, once people are in love they are putty in the hands of their loved ones. As their loved ones don't happen to be around, it means they are putty in the hands of the local church. Over the subsequent months the new converts can be drained of their energy, their time and their money. Their families and former friends are on the one hand neglected and on the other soon become targets for further soul hunting.

Whatever demands are made and however unreasonable the requests, it is all justified by reference to God. In the hands of the local church, God becomes a terrifying means of controlling people.

When the priest says to the new convert or when the new convert says to his or her partner, 'But God wants it to be done,' it takes a wise and brave person to answer, 'Well, I disagree.'

2 WHEN THE HONEYMOON IS OVER

When people fall in love they are often willing to be very flexible about their own identity. They are high on the experience of being close to someone and they want nothing to disturb that intimacy.

However, after a while, as the heady days of early romance spill into the bleaker days of everyday life, so their sense of identity becomes important again. After all, that is who they are, and surely if they are truly loved they will be accepted.

New converts remember the early days when church members visited them and spoke lovingly to them and were willing to welcome them with open arms. Then they spoke of forgiveness, the happiness of belonging to a group of people who didn't judge one another, the joy of belonging.

Now slowly the masks begin to slip and it's possible to

see the church members for real. Many of them are afraid of life with all its complicated feelings and desires.

Church life offers them an escape from adulthood. Clear boundaries are provided in terms of how they are expected to behave and what they are expected to believe. They are promised outside help and a ticket to heaven. It's a neat package for those finding it too painful to grow up.

DON'T DARE ROCK THE BOAT

It works, of course, if no one rocks the boat. Introduce newcomers who question too much or live too differently and they will find themselves rapidly mangled and unwelcome. Then the awful truth dawns that there is a price to pay for this so called 'unconditional' love, and that price is conformity.

Whether the church is an old fashioned church or modern, it has a culture of its own. Woe betide the person who questions or threatens it. It might as well be the Masonic Lodge or the Golf Club. What you have is a group of people sharing a common interest. In itself that is quite innocent, but what makes it potentially sinister is that the church club consists of people who claim they speak for God.

If you contradict them or present an alternative point of view they bring in their weaponry, the heavy guns which appear impressive but on closer inspection amount to very little indeed.

First they quote the Bible. Many of them don't begin to understand it, but as the old adage says a little knowledge is more dangerous than none at all! Then they lay claim to what God has told them that morning in their prayers, which usually is, coincidentally, merely a reinforcement of their own views and opinions.

Newcomers don't really stand a chance. They are

slowly led into submission and begin to learn the strange language of religious people. Instead of saying 'I think' they begin to say, 'The Lord says'; instead of 'I've decided to' they say 'God wants me to'; instead of 'I don't agree with that' they say, 'It's not the Lord's will'.

It becomes apparent to those able to hold on to their identity and their intellect that this is a form of brainwashing and mind control. Yet, horrors upon horrors, it's happening not in some strange cult, but in the respectable church at the top of the road!

THE LADYBIRD GOSPEL

What may also begin to stick in the throat is the simplistic and offensive way that the Christian faith is taught and required to be believed.

At colleges and schools, in pubs and clubs, people today have a sensible and quite pragmatic approach to the old Bible stories. Adam and Eve are given their rightful place as fictional characters in a legendary play about our beginnings. The tale of the virgin birth is seen as a religious way of putting a spotlight on Jesus; the resurrection as a poetic symbol of that evolutionary spirit that will not be crushed, of a love and hope that can face and survive anything and everything.

Such an understanding frees up the Bible to be of some use in today's world. Some of its stories become fun; they make sense and preserve insights. The message at the heart of them is known and lived out in people's lives every single moment across the world.

However, in your local church there is no such freedom. The priest and the people expect you to swallow the lot as fact, truth, actual happenings. Adam and Eve walked in the garden and set the whole ball rolling. Mary was a virgin. The tomb was empty.

The child-centred approach taken in Sunday School is continued in the regular sermon slot. Educational wisdom that children move from a rigid view of truth to a more abstract one as they grow up is lost on the church. It's as though the priest expected his congregation to believe that the Father Christmas story was true and rejected them if they didn't.

The newcomer who questions such an approach in the church may be tolerated for a while but soon the notice to quit arrives, either formally or in the body language of the ones who once smiled.

PETTY POLITICS

Perhaps you have managed to swallow the dogma and conform to the lifestyle; you are launched into the church community. Prepare for a rude awakening! The church, like most other communities, is a minefield of petty power politics and protected interests. If you dare step on someone else's territory, then all hell will break loose.

I remember once inviting a timid and gentle newcomer to do the flowers in our prayer chapel at harvest. This had been the domain of two 'old timers' before, one of whom went storming round the church holding the entire festival to ransom by her emotional outburst. From that day onwards she cold shouldered the newcomer, who felt violated and confused.

However, it doesn't just end at flowers. Every job in the church is 'possessed' by someone and woe betide anyone else who interferes.

Perhaps no office is so jealously guarded as that of churchwarden. It is a depressing experience attending a gathering of churchwardens; even more depressing to look more closely at their role on the ground. Many have held the position for years. Often it allows those who have difficulties with their own self-esteem to hold a position unavailable to them in ordinary life. Inflated by their sense of status they use their power unkindly and to the detriment of others.

The church is littered with those holding a title or carrying a job. This is no simple warm-hearted, open-handed community. It is shot through with ugly dynamics which the priest and the bishop know only too well and are either involved in themselves or struggle to contain and hide from public scrutiny.

THE PRIEST, MINISTER OR CHURCH LEADER

If it's not the people who cause you difficulty it may well be the minister.

I have met many ministers. A very small number of them were safe human beings. The rest I wouldn't trust with my life or my soul. The problem lies not with their own inadequacies but with their inability to own them and understand their lives and beliefs in relation to other forms of knowledge. Their involvement in and use of religion is often a means of easing their own pain and insecurity. They lack personal insight and so are clumsy in their understanding of others.

I remember vividly being shown how to conduct a marriage rehearsal. The bride asked if she could wear her veil down for the first part of the service. The priest was adamant in his refusal which reduced the bride to tears. He then threw down his book and stormed off to the choir stalls where he sat in silence, until the bride was forced to accept his decision. When I protested I was told to be silent because he was the voice of God in the parish and what he said must be obeyed. No one dared resist him, not even the bishop.

I hear a continual stream of similar horror stories: the vicar who wouldn't marry a dying man to the woman with whom he had lived for ten years because 18 years before she had been divorced; the vicar who wouldn't baptise a baby because the parents were unmarried; the vicar who would not speak with those of other faiths because as far as he was concerned they were from the devil; the vicar who turned away a dying man from his door because it was too late at night for him to be disturbed; the vicar who, the next day, threw away the floral tributes laid at his church in memory of Princess Diana, because he didn't agree with such public mourning. The list is endless.

The stories illustrate personality types that are threatened and insecure and that are uncompassionate in the application of their views. What is frightening is that these are the very people to whom others go in their most vulnerable states. At times of difficulty or tragedy people turn to a priest for help. If only they knew what a perilous choice they had made.

One couple told me how they attended their parish church for the first time only to hear the vicar at the start of the service, in his notices, ask everyone to sign the petition at the back of the church to try and stop a celebration of gay sexuality taking place in the cathedral. It doesn't take long for such brutal assumptions and disregard for other people's views and lives to cause offence.

3 BEHIND THE MASKS

One of the most obnoxious discoveries awaiting the new-comer is to find that while on the one hand there is the pretence of 'saintliness', in reality life inside the church is exactly the same as life outside. But let's be clear. It's not the human weaknesses and mistakes that stink, it's the hypocrisy.

During my time working within the established church, I met churchgoers who had had multiple affairs, married men living double lives with homosexual lovers or clubbing it in Soho, women who had affairs with abortions to match, policemen who had deliberately lied in court to frame the innocent in order to gain promotion, people stealing from the church in order to support secret addictions. Then there were the irritable, the greedy, the boring, the stuffed shirts, the artificial, the gossip merchants, the rude and the insensitive. Alongside them also were the kinder, gentler and more well balanced sort of people, together making up a mixed bag of ordinary life.

Of course the same applied to clergy, who did all the same sort of things as everyone else. There was no difference, how could there have been? I knew priests who had slept with their parishioners of both sexes, taken drugs, stolen from the collection plate, visited prostitutes, been addicts of one form or another, had abused children in their parish; others were arrogant, opinionated, ambitious, power hungry or 'holier than thou'. Alongside them there were others who were warmer, more considerate and showed greater understanding and care.

My purpose in writing all of this is not to be sensationalist, only truthful; my intention is not to be judgmental, only descriptive. The ordinary, sensible person in the street knows that everyone faces the same struggles, and is not surprised when people run into problems. The Christian community is meant to be on hand to help and support us through our times of brokenness and difficulty.

Nor is there surprise that objectionable people as well as pleasant ones call themselves Christians. After all, we meet a mixed bunch in our everyday lives, so why not in church?

However, what newcomers learn to their horror is that church people play by different rules. At church, the order of the day is to pretend that those attending, and their priests, are in some way 'different', the good ones, filled with the Holy Spirit, becoming holier by the day, setting an example to the world, shining as lights to those around them.

In order to maintain this pretence, great pressure is exerted within the church to be dishonest. The rule is: Keep your real problems to yourself. Keep who you are, what you feel, what you believe, to yourself if it in any way differs from the norm. If someone's unpleasantness is obvious to all (as in rudeness or arrogance), everyone else has to pretend it doesn't exist.

Some of the situations I've referred to above are in themselves not surprising. If you are well versed in life you should rarely be shocked at what people tell you about their lives. However, what the newcomer will continue to find hard to swallow is that the people I've mentioned above, priests or church members, chose to hide their own wounded personalities from everyone else. No one in the church knew what they got up to alone.

Perhaps that was excusable in the interests of their privacy and their desire for space and healing. What made it inexcusable was the sight and sound of these same people judging and condemning others with similar difficulties. No doubt this was another symptom of their paranoia about being discovered themselves. If they made enough fuss about someone else the spotlight would be away from them.

Beware! In entering a church community, you enter a group of people who are playing many invisible games. You are wrong to think that this is the warm, welcoming environment in which you will find acceptance, resources for your struggles and healing. Rather the vultures are waiting to dive and feed on the unsuspecting innocent who makes the mistake of being honest. They will increase their own sense of goodness and increase their own prestige on your flesh, while burying their own darkness deeper and deeper within.

THE GREAT COVER UP

Bishops and priests reading these pages will be nodding to themselves with a wry smile. They know about many of the messes, potential scandals and crises which litter the church, but their job is to deny that they exist. As in any big company, they don't like bad press.

The troubleshooting approach goes something like this. First rule: Keep it private. The bishop or priest doesn't want to know. The second rule involves damage limitation: if it becomes known, try and cover it up or squeeze the issue back in its box while publicly adopting the 'flannel and gloss' treatment. The third rule involves crisis management: if it's all out, wash your hands of all responsibility, knowledge or involvement and scapegoat the individuals as much as possible.

As the honeymoon period fades, such happenings leave newcomers with gaping mouths. They look with astonishment as once loved, cherished, and doted upon members of Christ's community are chucked into the dustbin. Earlier talk of forgiveness, turning the other cheek, love, healing, reconciliation, seeking out the lost, reaching out to the broken, accepting and caring for one another and not throwing the first stone, is heard no more.

In fact the most bizarre thing is the deafening silence which surrounds the whole issue — backed up by ferocious condemnations should a word be breathed on the subject. The make-up artists get to work piling it on thick and colourful, burying the realities and the heartaches of true life deep, deep down. All important is the preservation of the mask. After all, tears might make the mascara run!

AND WHAT IF IT'S YOU?

The mouth might gape open as you watch all of this happening to someone else, but what if it was you?

Perhaps you'd had contact with the church because your father had died. Following the funeral the 'Let's get his soul' campaign had swung into action and all sorts of attention had been heaped upon you. Lonely and hurting, you were an easy target for such offers of love and care and the warm and accepting community of the church appeared an inviting and cosy place to belong.

Perhaps you'd enjoyed the friendship and the laughter of the other church members after the services, had been invited to their homes for meals and on outings. Perhaps the sermons and prayers which described the beauty of being a part of God and one another filled the cruel gap of losing a parent.

Perhaps, having grown confident in the community, it felt quite appropriate and an act of trust and faith to tell the churchwarden or the priest that you were gay and that you were going to bring your gay partner along on Sunday to worship.

Perhaps then it was you who was exposed to all the dark and brutal prejudice and rejection of a community too threatened by life to be able to see you, love you or accept you any more. Suddenly you had become expendable and all that was left was the waiting for the binmen to pass.

AND WHAT IF YOU ARE IN HIDING?

Perhaps you are one of the lucky ones who, having seen it happen to someone else, has been warned. You still go and still perform the charade of smiling and laughing and joking with all the people at the back of the church, while all the time harbouring your truth in the privacy of your heart.

It may be that you have a money problem or are in trouble with the police. You may be divorced, or living with someone, or are a single parent. Perhaps you're having an affair, or are a transvestite. You may attend Alcoholics Anonymous or be a compulsive gambler. Your evenings may be spent at the local lesbian club. You may take cannabis, attend seances, watch porno movies. You may swear, cheat money out of the DSS, fiddle your books. You may have pierced nipples and tattoos galore.

There could be many things you get up to, some fine but not seen to be 'respectable' at church, and others suspect. Some people are trapped in forms of behaviour that are not helpful for them or others; some have grown to a point of self-confidence where they are able to own and celebrate what makes them who they are.

However, if the behaviour is destructive or it's alternative or it doesn't fit in with the neat and tidy expectations of religious people, then watch out. Your choice is secrecy or rejection or, of course, the more sensible and healthy approach which is to choose to leave while the going's good.

THE ESCAPE DOOR
SWINGS SLOWLY SHUT

It doesn't take long for the community to attach itself to you and your psyche. The newcomer is exposed from day one to little subtle messages dropped along the way about loyalty, sticking together, God's chosen few, beating off Satan, keeping together those who have strayed. As the days pass it becomes harder and harder to escape. Each route is blocked. Every door is filled with an insincere smiling face, each tactic is scuppered by the campaign to keep him or her on board.

There's not much one can do. Either stay on board the silent phantom express or create a showdown by exposing the truth. Few have the courage for the showdown so the train forever chugs along on its empty way.

4 THE KIDDIES' CLUB

The trouble starts when you put two or three people together. It's as though a virus emerges and begins to attack the individuals concerned.

People who were once strong and self-assured, who knew themselves and had sorted out their lives, are suddenly thrown into a state of panic and self-doubt. Now an invisible force called 'the group' begins to gain power and to demand respect and loyalty.

This happens in any group, but in a religious group it's even more dangerous because the power exerted by the group is renamed 'God' or 'Jesus'.

Slowly a new language replaces the energetic and stimulating chatter of independent adults. Phrases like, 'Well, God wouldn't want us to', 'It's not God's will', 'But Jesus would be hurt' are used, meaning, 'Well, the group wouldn't think much of that', 'It's not what this group stands for', or 'But people would be hurt'. Slowly the group curls itself around individuals until they either sur-render and are squeezed into conformity or they perish.

Regrettably it's what happens in so many marriages, where the individuality of both partners is watered down by the expectations and requirements of the other. Multiply this many times in the dynamics of the group and you end up with a kindergarten of adults.

YOU CYNIC!

Perhaps you think I'm being unnecessarily hard. But think of the harm that becoming involved in such a group can do to a person. For years you have slowly matured and taken the brave journey of processing life and making sense of your situation. Then along comes the glory train promising an easy ride to heaven with cosy passengers. It can look as though the lottery has passed your way and you sink everything in the gamble. Then some way down the track, if you're truly lucky, you realise you've been conned. Getting off is hard.

TELLTALE CLUES

There are certain things which should cause a twinge of concern to the newcomer. For instance, what happens in worship?

In most churches, although the form and style varies, certain ingredients are common. There are words spoken or sung. There is action (receiving communion, or just changing bodily positions), and there is a sermon or talk.

Of course there are the age-old questions which the newcomer might well ask, like why it all happens in such a stylised way and why the music is the type it is and why every week, even in more lively worship, the same things occur again and again.

But the more worrying question is why the words of the service aren't turned into actions. How can someone pray for harmony and then continue to ignore someone with whom they are angry? How can the peace be offered in handshakes and hugs around the church when afterwards there are all sorts of people who won't talk to one another?

Why is it that people can speak of unity and all eat the bread at communion and then despise and criticise each other over coffee, following the service?

How can they listen to the story of the woman caught in adultery and then condemn someone they know in that situation? How can they pray for the poor and give no time or money to charity? How can they read about God's concern for the oppressed and then mock and ridicule anyone involved in Amnesty International? How can they recite the call to love and yet reject and condemn so many people in society who don't fit into their nice neat way of believing and behaving?

The list is endless and it forms a chasm between the fine words of the service and the way the members of the congregation live their lives. If this were the result of weakness, then understanding would be needed. However, the people concerned are puffed up with their own self-righteousness. By feeding on religious words and guzzling communion they are fat with self-satisfaction that at least they have done God's will.

THE LONG, LONG SPOUT

Perhaps the most gruelling thing of all is the charade that takes place during the sermon. Young ministers spend days perfecting their offering; theological colleges spend weeks preparing their students for the task and what at the end of the day do we have? Someone being given the chance to air his personal views and prejudices about Jesus, the Bible, life and society — yet all in the name of God. Meanwhile the congregation are meant to be lapping it all up.

It doesn't take long for the wise person to realise two salutary things. The first and more serious point is that this process has very often little if anything to do with God. It is much more an attempt by the priest to force his (or her) church into believing his (or her) way. The second rather amusing point is that probably no one learns or remembers anything from any sermon ever, and that most people daydream through the sermon slot.

If you think this is untrue, take your average church-goer who has listened to at least a thousand sermons. Here's betting that they wouldn't be able to answer even the simplest questions about their faith.

THE GREAT MISTAKE

You are in danger for as long as you take the people, the language and the beliefs at face value. If, instead, you keep your wits about you, protect your own understanding and wisdom at all costs and put every one of your experiences through your own filtering system, then you should survive.

In a way, that process is what most people do routinely with their experiences in life; but somehow if they get sucked into a church they drop their defences in the belief that this at least is a safe place. They think that here they can be open and honest about themselves and love and acceptance will surround them. How wrong they are.

Groups, religious or otherwise, have a fairly consistent way of behaving. They have an identity, boundaries, a culture and a pattern of life. Threaten it, challenge it, question it or resist it and the ugly defensive power of the group will be directed your way.

BUT SURELY JESUS COMES INTO THIS, DOESN'T HE?

I remember during one Easter period trying to arrange a service which was as near as possible to being like the one Jesus shared with his friends the night before he died. Many in the church were most offended because it was different to their normal Communion service. I explained that I was trying to remind us all of how it had all begun. The response was astonishing. 'But we don't care if it's more like what Jesus did, we just want our normal communion service.' This said it all.

I venture to suggest that most of what happens in church life and is taught by the church has very little to do with Jesus. Instead, the years of tradition, habit and custom have obscured his life and his memory. What remains is the practice of a mega multinational religious company, popularly referred to as the church, which markets itself and its version of religion with its accumulated wealth and widespread power.

As long as you realise this and enter a church with your eyes open and you are sufficiently interested to watch this particular group practise its version of religion, then it might be of value. If, however, you are looking for the real thing, trying to get in touch with Jesus, to experience the beauty, mystery and power of the spiritual, then your search must continue beyond the walls of the church.

I used to offend my former congregations regularly by saying that they might have come to church that morning to find God, to talk with Jesus, to feel they had done their duty, make God happy through their prayers and their attendance, but how wrong they were.

If they wanted to find God and talk with Jesus, the church would be the last place to find him. If they wanted to make God happy, prayers and church attendance came at the bottom of the list of priorities and it certainly had nothing to do with duty. Those things were probably more to do with the enjoyment of their chosen routine and a chance for them to catch up on the gossip.

No, the Spirit of God can never be contained within the walls, systems and insular groups we set up. Thankfully God defies our every attempt at control. Our assumptions, prejudices and expectations are shattered when we find God in the feisty, sad lives of the street beggars, in the raw honesty of prostitution, in the earthy language of pub banter, in the beauty of gay love, in the meandering thoughts of an agnostic, in the messy, untidy and wonderful world of reality.

The true community of God has no walls and is much the safest place to be. It is wherever you are, whenever you are. It is with everyone and anyone. It is all and everything, no one excluded, no one abandoned, no one dumped. The church of God is the cathedral of the universe.

In the intertwining of all our lives, in the multitude of conversations, in the passing smiles and regular humdrum pattern of life is God, the Spirit, prayer and worship.

The church building itself often offers a refuge, a shelter and a hiding place from truth; that's why priests should stop mollycoddling the faithful and instead preach, 'On your bikes!'

5 PLEASE GIVE GENEROUSLY

I hold the image in my mind of an Orthodox priest in Moscow receiving an endless stream of poorly dressed women who passed him requests for prayer and stuffed wads of roubles into his bag. The church gleamed with gold and jewels, while the homes in which the worshippers lived were hovels. All over the world the poor languish while the church holds immense wealth and capital reserves. This country is no exception. The church is responsible for billions of pounds of assets and capital. The mind boggles.

Another image that lives with me is of the tiny church where St Francis used to preach. He spoke of poverty and simplicity and his life was the expression of that. Go to Assisi now and you will find his original humble church encased in a multiple level cathedral built in his honour. In the Holy Land many of the original sites marking events in the stories surrounding Jesus are now entombed in magnificent and elaborate buildings.

It's a perfect modern example of how we deceive ourselves into believing that we continue the memory of a person even though we may be destroying everything that person represented.

Exquisite cathedrals and the thousands of churches are a distraction from, even a contradiction of, the life of Jesus. They exist as symbols of power and prestige, of money and control, of the corruption of a religious system gone off the rails.

Don't misunderstand; I love beautiful buildings. I adore stained glass and the richly woven robes of the clergy. I love art in all its wonderful forms. However, if these beauties are to be pursued it is a task for other organisations or groups and not the church, at least not yet.

There can be no justification for spending billions of pounds erecting and maintaining buildings which are empty and unused for most of the week. How shocking to think that if you calculated how often the churches up and down the land were actually used in a week it would amount to only a few hours. That is why most of them are damp and musty places, costing thousands to repair and being of no use or relevance to the majority of the people who live around them.

NOW PLEASE SUPPORT YOUR LOCAL CHURCH AND LET THE POOR STARVE

In almost every service there is the clinking of coins as the collection plate takes its lazy journey through the congregation. Appeals are constantly made for money and some people don't twig what's happening for a long time. In many people's minds to give to the church is to give to God. The gift is to help where help is needed most and that means, for most people, the poor and needy.

However, hardly any money at all, and in many cases none at all, goes from the collection plate to the poor. Instead there are the countless headings on the budget sheet to be funded. A great chunk has to be given to the regional church office. More chunks go on repairs, heating, insurance, printing, supplies. At the end of the day, perhaps £20,000 or £50,000 or £80,000 or more later, it's all gone. The poor and the needy haven't had a look in.

Let's be clear. Money given to the church is not for God, it's to bolster up a human system of religion which is so greedy that it is rarely satisfied.

Of course, there may be special collections for specific appeals but in comparison with the overall expenditure these pale into insignificance. They are the cosmetics to give the appearance of charity.

CORRUPTION AND CANT

The trouble is that you can't ever win an argument with religious people because they have two weapons. If you challenge them from a religious angle they say they have to be wise according to worldly standards. If then you challenge them by worldly standards they conveniently start spouting religion.

When I was vicar of a large parish in south east London my first task was to stop one end of the church from collapsing. A large sum of money was needed. The parish had in the past raised considerable chunks of money to buy land and construct a vicarage which was now to be sold. I asked the regional church office if a proportion of the proceeds of the sale could come to the parish to help with the repair. They played the legal card, answering 'No'. Apparently church law had changed, effectively taking ownership of the vicarages and sites away from all the parishes. Irrespective of the fact that the parish had paid for the vicarage, not even a small amount would be made available. The worldly card had been played.

Then it transpired that the Church Council still owned a strategic strip of land bordering the road which was crucial if the land was going to be sold for the highest price. The diocese advised us that it was worth £20,000.

A surveyor on our Council pointed out that it had a

'ransom' value and was worth considerably more. We mentioned this to the diocese and they informed us that the diocesan surveyor had advised them to raise their offer to £60,000. We then took independent advice and were told that our land was worth commercially between £120,000 and £150,000.

The diocese then played the religious card. How wrong of us to go to an independent surveyor when their surveyor was acting as a Christian for both the diocese and the parish! How could we be causing such conflict by asking for more than we were being offered? How could we be so greedy as to want so much money for it anyway? And so on.

The mixture of moral, religious and worldly attack was manipulative and corrupt. We stuck to our guns saying we were happy for there to be negotiation between our surveyor and theirs. After endless meetings, personal attacks and a long-lasting stalemate, compromise was reached between their £60,000 and our £120,000, resulting in a payment of £90,000.

I should add that we gave £9000 of it away to various charities and spent the rest on the repair of the church. However, because I resisted the church authorities from both a religious and worldly angle I was thereafter branded a troublemaker.

BACKHANDERS

In one parish I was surprised by two things. The first was when a lady contacted me saying that it had been her practice all through her life to donate 10% of her income to the church. She had spoken about this in confidence with a priest and he had arranged with her to make the cheque out personally to him. He would then see that it went to the church. I looked through all the records and consulted the treasurer to see if approximately £150 a month had been paid in over the years. The answer was 'No'.

A little later, while consulting a group who wished to use the church premises, I was asked whether I wanted the cheque for £200 for their hire of the church to be made payable to me personally, as the other priest had done.

Slowly I became aware that there was lots of money floating around which should have been going into the church funds and had been diverted.

Not that it was limited to the clergy. Churchwardens too put their fingers in the pot while counting, as did some other officials if the chance was presented to them. Sometimes it was their only way to support an addiction, sometimes it was to bolster the family income.

People putting their money innocently into the collection plate in the church do so trusting that it will be handled honestly and be used lovingly within a system where there is a proper balance between religious principles and worldly wisdom. Sadly, this is often far from the truth.

GO ON, SUPPORT THE CLUB!

There's nothing wrong with paying for a way of life you enjoy. If the church building, its music and way of life is up your street then dig deep and pay your subscription to keep the show on the road. But don't muddle this up with doing your Christian duty. If you want to give to God, if you want to care for the poor, the weak and the oppressed, then giving to the church is a completely ineffective way of doing it.

I reckon if God was to send down a list of approved charities, it would be likely to include development agencies like Oxfam and Save the Children. Christian Aid might get a look in or the Red Crescent, as might some of those often debated charities which support Aids patients, the homeless, the unemployed, transsexuals and so on — the list is endless. I don't reckon the Church of England or the Roman Catholic Church or any organised religious group would get a look in!

6 COLD, HARD STONE

There is nothing more threatening to a settled community than a breath of fresh air. The old timers kid themselves with dreams along the lines of 'If only the church was full of young people' — 'If only more came for baptism' — 'If only . . .'

The priest encourages people to bring their friends and work colleagues, promising to all a warm and heartfelt welcome. I even heard one bishop try and prepare the congregations at a confirmation for the possibility that newcomers bring with them new ideas.

Perish the thought! Your local church is steeped in tradition. It oozes out of every corner, every practice, every service. From major things to the most trivial, those terrible words are rehearsed, 'Well, it's always been done like this.'

In some ways if the areas of rigidity were minor perhaps it wouldn't matter. However, tradition, habit and prejudice run through every part of the community, encasing it in stone, with as little flexibility as Mount Everest.

THE PETRIFYING PROCESS

Ordinary people are unique individuals bringing with them their own flavours of humanity and their own rich and various experiences of life. As such they act, think, feel and believe differently. Wonderful, one might think! What an opportunity to refresh, expand and stimulate the community!

Not so. You've probably heard the old stories about how Medusa could turn a person to stone with one look! Well, the church hasn't quite got that power yet, but it tries. From the moment you walk in the door an invisible process begins to turn the beautiful, warm, mysterious you into a stone dummy that fills space but affects as little as possible.

THE SEARCH FOR TRUTH

A lot is spoken about truth in churches. Most churchgoers think they have some form of monopoly over it. Yet their truth exists in a closely patrolled area they create for themselves. It is a self-contained world, almost like an island, and they pretend that there is nothing more to life than what they experience there.

The fact that there are so many different countries, so many different continents and so many different planetary systems – that there are so many different faiths and philosophies and cultures – that there are so many people whose approach to life is different – this is dismissed out of hand.

The party line is simple. If something is not as we think it should be, it's wrong and of the devil.

If the newcomers have alert minds and an enquiring manner, it doesn't take long for them to become annoyed. They ask awkward questions, and present information which contradicts the accepted view; they persist in pressing boundaries and won't be fobbed off.

Churchgoers employ various tactics to cope in such situations. Lines of defence include, 'Well, you're quite young in the faith, but in time you'll see,' or, 'It's a matter of trust; our human minds can't understand everything,' or, 'That's where faith comes in. Look at Thomas: Jesus said, "Blessed are those who don't see and yet still believe".'

It's a clever but deadly mix of two ingredients. On the one hand is the pretence that the faith is all worked out; that it's logical, consistent, proved by the Bible, and can be debated convincingly. Then on the other hand, when you come across a great gap in the evidence, in common sense, in rationale, you fill it up conveniently with an appeal to faith and belief.

KEEP DIGGING

Don't be fobbed off and don't let the glory blazers get away with it. Keep pressing at the boundaries of their understanding and believing. Keep asking what they mean by the words they speak and what experiences lie underneath those words.

The trouble is, you are often dealing with fairly vulnerable people who have shielded themselves from life with their religion. Start asking them to come clean and emerge and you may well not be prepared for their reactions. These can verge on the hysterical, coming out in tantrums, anger, threats or abuse, or they will direct the full fury of their feelings on to you, claiming that you are from the devil or that you are possessed or calling your entire character into question.

However, if you press on undeterred, you will begin to find that the religious words people use are only a front for their own thoughts and prejudices. There are all sorts of explanations as to why they need to dress them up in this way, but largely it boils down to their own lack of confidence and insecurity. It certainly sounds more important to be able to say, 'It's God's will,' rather than,

'I think . . .'

Of course if people want to delude themselves in this way and it works for them, perhaps there's no problem. But religion rarely finishes at the individual's door. As churchgoers are an insecure breed who bolster up their own identities with religion, so it becomes necessary for them to seek safety in numbers.

The more people there are doing the same thing, going to church in the same way and coming out with the same beliefs, the more those involved can relax into believing that it's all bona fide and sensible and they are not insane.

You only have to look at the practice of religion the world over, in every faith on every continent, to witness the frenzied activity of religious nutcases trying to convert the world into believing their way, on the basis that they alone have the real, absolute and only truth.

WHAT DID THEY SAY?

Sometimes there are moments of insight when someone in the church gives their world view away. Inside my bag of throw-away lines that I've collected from churchgoers over the years is this choice selection:

'We just had sex when we wanted children. That's what it's for, isn't it?'

'You're bad if you work on a Sunday.'

'Giving to the poor has nothing to do with God. It's the communists that started all of that.'

'We don't want a person like that in church, they're probably on drugs.'

'I didn't come to church to hear about missionaries being killed.'

'I never come to a baptism service — there are too many strangers there.'

If you go to church, sitting right next to you might be someone who is racist or hung up about gays; someone who believes the Bible literally or who thinks Hindus are devil worshippers. That may not affect you, but it would if you happened to have been born in Africa, if your wife is a Hindu or if you didn't happen to believe Adam and Eve were historical people. And it's worse if people around you start to dress up their prejudice or viewpoint in religious terms, claiming that the Bible backs them up and that God condemns homosexuality and all other faiths and that 'If you were a committed Christian, a born again believer, if you really knew Jesus, you would understand.'

PUT YOUR TOE IN FIRST

Of course every church is different in that each priest and each catchment area produces a different feel, as well as each church having a particular historical tradition. If you are clued up and know what to look out for and what questions to ask you can assess the potential damage factor of being involved.

Yet I remain amazed at people's innocence. They attend one service and come away saying, 'Oh, the vicar was so lovely and friendly and there were guitars,' or some such shallow assessment of the place and people. What I always want to ask is, 'But what about their beliefs? Are they hardliners, fundamentalists, evangelicals? What makes them tick?'

THE TICK FACTOR

While it can be confusing trying to interpret religio-speak, it can also be enlightening. A person's beliefs are a window through which one can look at the heart and soul. Ask them to speak about their faith and very soon a picture can form as to what you can expect from this person, how they might react in various situations and most important of all whether they pose a threat to you or not.

At times people will speak about ideals which in reality they can't live up to or practise, but again the discerning listener remains aware of the credibility factor. Those who have the neatest, clearest, simplest and most precise manner of believing are usually those with most to hide and most to be feared. The trouble is they are also the most convincing.

So make good use of those toes! Ask away, question everyone extensively, listen avidly and give nothing away of yourself. Sus out the enemy; if they turn out to be potential friends all to the good. However, if dangers lurk by every pew or chair you can escape while the going's good.

ON BALANCE

While personal experimentation is always attractive, this book is to warn people about the process from my experience. True, you may be the sort of person who will fit in well and enjoy the pattern of parish life, or you may be one of the few who strike gold and find a genuinely accepting and nourishing community.

What is more likely is that you will find, time and time again, churches harbouring paranoid individuals with narrow minds and burgeoning prejudices in whose company you would most certainly perish.

PART TWO
WINNING THE LOTTERY OF FAITH

7 IT'S ALL IN A WORD

'God said to me this morning . . .'

When someone comes out with a statement like that you can see the quizzical look cross the face of a new-comer. The language goes on:

'But the Lord has told me . . .'

'I must ask God whether I should or not.'

'I live my life by the Bible, because it's God's word.'

'Jesus came to me last night.'

'It's not me, it's the Lord.'

'I couldn't do anything without God's power.'

'I've given my heart to Jesus and now he lives inside me.'

Certain Christians have a strange and disconcerting way of turning ordinary life into what sounds like mystical and miraculous experience. The desire to do so isn't surprising, after all, life can be very tedious. Spice it up with invisible powers, a cosmic purpose and a royal visitor and it takes on a whole new meaning.

However, for someone with eyes to see, living by religious fantasy is as dissatisfying as living through Hollywood or Disney films or comic strips. What is more, life itself can be marvellous and mysterious without having to pep it up.

ROLL ON THE INTERPRETER

So what are they going on about? If you are brave enough to corner such a person with precise questions, you can quickly learn the art of translation yourself. What does 'God said to me this morning . . .' actually mean? Does it mean there was a knock at the door and God strolled in? Does it mean that there was a puff of smoke and God appeared? Does it mean there was a voice out of the blue?

What was the experience that the person had? The experience comes first and then the person tries to find language with which to describe what happened to them. Unfortunately, instead of stumbling around and putting it into words that make sense for them, the church steps in and gives ready made phrases and convenient words that the newcomer quickly learns and parrots.

Press them on exactly what happened and don't be satisfied until you can picture the event. Resist any vague or fudgy language.

What will begin to emerge is something like this. The person was sitting alone reading the Bible as the church had suggested they should. In it he/she reads something that rings a bell, strikes a chord, applies to something with which he/she is involved. Perhaps it even seems to suggest an answer, give a clue, point in a direction. The person has a sense that someone knows about the situation and is providing some help. Indeed what a wonderful thing that would be. He/she is not alone. Suddenly this great big world is not quite such a lonely place. God is there and is close at hand.

The person feels excited inside. A warm feeling rises within them. They go away with the words, 'God spoke to me this morning' ringing in their ears.

SO WHAT STAR SIGN ARE YOU?

'Fine,' one might say. 'No harm done.' Possibly that's true. On the other hand, if you let it go at face value you have not seen the deception. This is no divine intervention, no message direct from heaven. This is a very human experience repeated the world over.

Millions turn hungrily to read their stars every day in papers and magazines. Others consult Mystic Meg and her colleagues. Some feel something connect in a book, a film, on television, in a song or through a coincidence. All of these people are finding that something outside them has been meaningful in some way.

Of course if we assess the experience honestly we are being bombarded by external stimuli every day of our lives. Most of it is irrelevant and unhelpful; a small proportion creates some sort of link.

People who are susceptible to that link and live their lives under its spell are in for a rough ride. As we all know, some of the links can be very sinister and unhelpful. Some people have lived in terror for years or just been bugged uncomfortably because of what a fortune teller told them.

Religious links can be just as sinister. The links made in the Bible have caused people to do all sorts of crazy and cruel things. Some have left unbelieving partners, or rejected their wayward children, or thrown their families into chaos by leaving secure jobs, or joined suspect groups and rejected lifelong friends.

THE ROULETTE WHEEL

Every time these Christians read their Bible or pray, they spin the roulette wheel. Sometimes it will fall happily on an innocuous verse or a constructive thought. At other times it will precipitate damaging decisions and unpredictable behaviour.

The problem lies in the absence of any objective or external arbiter. There is no religious ombudsman to whom individuals or their families can go. Fred turns up saying that God has told him that morning to leave his engineering job and begin Christian work. Who can resist God?

The empowered person, who has learnt the art of translation and can stand up to religio-speak, isn't intimidated. It's not God they are dealing with, it's Fred.

HE'S JUST CRACKED!

It's tempting to write off religio-speak altogether, but if you can pass through the threatened stage and disarm the language, then, as I indicated earlier, it says a lot about the person concerned.

It tells us perhaps that Fred is unhappy in his present job or feels unfulfilled in his career or life so far, or has hidden goals or unrealised dreams. There are so many possibilities. Knowledge of Fred would enable someone to translate his religious language into everyday insights that showed how he was feeling about his life.

People who go heavily into religion and start having

wild and weird spiritual experiences need to be understood and helped through what is a life crisis. They need
to be taken seriously. That does not mean that you should
take on board their language or be taken in by the God
talk, but you should try and see through the windows it
all provides to the hearts of the people concerned.

The trouble is that such people or experiences can
often be quite extreme and off-putting. Those involved
go on and on about it, delirious with conversion fever and
eager to validate what they believe is happening to them
by getting you on board.

JOURNEY TO THE
CENTRE OF THE SOUL

It would be of great help if education included slightly more
about just how complex our personalities are and what
goes on inside us emotionally, and why. Very often we
remain clueless about the most amazing life-form that we
will ever be as close to, namely ourselves. We can learn the
wizardry of computers and achieve scientific feats that leave
us breathless, but still be uneducated about how we work.

This is why religion has such power over us. What we
don't realise is that religio-speak can unlock the hidden
treasures and darkest secrets of our lives. When used
properly it can provide a language with which we can tap
into our longings and our terrors, our tears and our joy.
It can give us the ability to discover and to talk about
hitherto unreached areas within ourselves.

This is its potential, but in most cases, because it is misunderstood, its followers rarely leave the nursery and
continue to use language with the range of a toddler.

THE FRIGHTENED CHILD
WITHIN

Just look at the phrase, 'I live my life by the Bible'. There are many people who just find growing up too hard and too lonely. As kids there were always adults to keep the boundaries, to point us in the right direction, but hit the problems of later life and it's up to you.

Decisions and choices vie for attention — and it's not just what dress or tie to wear. We have to decide which career move to make, whether to propose, what house to buy, where to live, whether to have an affair, whether to have a tumour removed, how to cope with an unwanted pregnancy and so on.

Wow! Where's someone who can give us the answer? Mum and Dad have lost their role, teachers are a faded memory, so it's God that gets lumbered. 'God will tell me what to do and his word will show me the way. All I have to do is find out and follow his will.'

It's so enticing to believe that God has a perfect plan for our lives, a constantly updating 'best' for each one of us, and that all we have to do is pray enough, ask enough, seek enough and all will be revealed.

What happens is one of two things. Either people are led up the garden path by randomly selecting signals or leads which they interpret as 'God's will'. This can lead to tragedy for them, or others involved. Or, they manage to manipulate the guidance that God has given to fit their own ideas.

The problem with this is that they won't take responsibility for the decision themselves and they resist every attempt to advise them otherwise with the pious words, 'Well, I don't expect that you will be able to understand, but it's God's will and you can't argue with God!'

If such people were to grow up, they would need to be helped to see how they were using religio-speak, how they had been duping themselves to cover over their fear of decision-making. Then they could be helped to begin to take the brave step of making up their own minds.

8 IF YOU WANT A HEALTHY BELIEF IN GOD, DON'T BELIEVE!

Most people make the basic mistake of thinking that they are meant to believe that the Christian faith is true.

When the church speaks about God, heaven and hell, the miracle stories, the virgin birth and the resurrection, they think they should accept it all as fact.

The trouble is that there are many priests today and many churches that have lost their way and simply declare that 'the Bible is fact!' How wrong they are! How they rubbish the treasures of the faith by doing so!

People don't realise just how dangerous words can be!

They have an experience of some kind. Perhaps they are sacked or have an accident or lose a parent. Something has happened. They then begin to speak about it. In fact everyone caught up in the experience will speak about it, and each will describe the events differently. Different words will be used, presenting different insights, feelings, interpretations, ideas and conclusions.

Anyone who has been involved with the courts or the

media will be able to tell you that trying to find out what exactly happened from the thousands of words spoken afterwards is an almost impossible task.

SORTING INTO BOXES

In trying to find out, it is useful to sort through the language. Into the first box we should place the language of fact: who was standing where and when, where they moved to, what they did and what they said.

The second box can then be filled up with the language about feelings: who was feeling what, what was the mood during the happening, what emotions were felt and how were they expressed.

The third box is for the language concerning people's views and interpretations, their ideas about the reasons and the causes for what happened from an earthly point of view.

The fourth box is for language that reflects on what can be learnt from the happening and how that wisdom can be protected in the future.

THE BIBLE'S BOXES

The problem is that when the Bible was written, people did not distinguish between such boxes and they used language in a way that many people today find loose and confusing.

For instance, the story of the Garden of Eden and Adam and Eve seems to be written as a factual account of how it all began. However, those writing it would have laughed if you had said to them, 'So this is what happened, is it?' They were writing religious stories and poetry to pass on their insights and wisdom. They had no idea what actually happened and as yet nor have we.

The silly arguments that take place about the miracle stories, the virgin birth and the resurrection are all in the same vein. If the biblical writers could speak today, they would tell us we were all mad and were missing the point completely.

But that is exactly the danger of language. How on earth can you be sure that your words will not be misunderstood, that what you are writing will not get mangled and reshaped? How can you stop Jesus' exciting and radical approach to religion being stuffed into a system of religion which is as dead and as spiritually bankrupt as the Judaism of Jesus' day? You can't!

RELIGIOUS LANGUAGE IS NOT MEANT TO BE TAKEN LITERALLY

We've made God into a teddy bear to be cuddled, Jesus into an SAS soldier who will rescue us, heaven into a Butlin's holiday camp for a good romp, and worship into a poor alternative to the pub.

We've reduced religio-speak to a banal and useless level that feeds the worst of our childishness and dependencies and we've corrupted the very resource whose function is to lift us to greater maturity and fulfilment. In fact the arena of argument in which silly people waste hours trying to prove that God exists and that Mary was a virgin ruins the wisdom and beauty of the Christian faith.

So tell the religio-nutcases to get lost and let's get serious about religion.

We need to understand one simple thing about religious language and we've cracked the code. *It is a way of talking about us, our experience, our lives and our situations.*

Now I know that some of you may have thrown your hands up in horror at this and be about to put the book down. Hang on a moment. I am not saying that God doesn't exist. What I am saying, though, is that if God does exist, then the religious language that we use does not and could not begin to describe God. God and all that we associate with God remains hidden from our observation. There are no facts about God, only feelings, interpretations and gathered ideas or wisdom.

SO WHAT IS THE CHURCH'S TEACHING ALL ABOUT?

Quite simply, the church's teaching describes us, as do our dreams which give us such provocative insights into what goes on inside our heads and how our subconscious processes our experience. So too it is with our religion.

The Bible stories and the beliefs that arise from them are almost like a series of daydreams. They are our fantasies and our imaginings. Some people manage to survive their lives by creating a world beside our world — rather as children need an imaginary friend or friends and spend many of their childhood years living with one foot in their imaginary world.

As adults we are more sophisticated than to have a comfort rag, but religion provides a neat alternative that is socially acceptable.

SO THEY'RE NO DARN GOOD THEN?

Quite the opposite! People's beliefs provide us with a treasure chest of knowledge about them and about ourselves. I say to people, 'Don't tell others your dreams.' It's like letting them look inside your box of secrets. So too your religion. Handle the material carefully.

If religio-speak is meant to protect what we have learnt from experiences by providing us with neat and easily remembered story lines, then it can be fun thinking about them. Perhaps it's like going to the trouble of peeling an orange to taste the glorious fruit inside.

In some of the following chapters I am going to peel away the rind of religion and get to the juice inside.

BUT WHAT ABOUT THE RIND?

For me and for most ordinary people I meet, the rind of religion is very bitter indeed. It makes the face screw up and the stomach ache. Of course it can be attractive when used for decoration and it can add zest when grated into life's dishes, but it is not meant to be food for our staple diets.

The biblical stories and doctrines about Jesus being perfect as the Son of God, and the second coming, heaven and hell, the body and blood of communion, are like poems. They should not be taken literally.

It's almost amusing to listen to adults talking about when the trumpet sounds at the second coming and how amazing it will be when the faithful are gathered up in the clouds. If only they could step back and listen to themselves! It's just as if they were talking about when Postman Pat was going to appear or if Cinderella was still happy in her marriage.

Adults become blasé about their childhood years and can mock cartoon and fairy story characters, but those years and that world hold such influence over many of us that we find it impossible to let it go. We import a new set of characters with staying power and dress them up a bit, but Disneymania rules supreme.

THE GREAT TEDDY BEAR

God fulfils a range of functions from being a Father Christmas replacement to a cuddly teddy bear. The devil is a useful bloke for passing the buck to. The Holy Spirit comes in handy for an extra boost of power when our confidence fails. Confession comes in handy if you want to forget about the past and heaven is a useful but rather deadly way of ignoring the urgency to make as much as is possible of your life here and now.

In fact, if you list all the devious ways we use religion which end up reducing and robbing us of our lives, we should be very angry with it indeed. But it appears like many things to which we are addicted, short term kicks and long term tragedy.

If you don't want to be hurt when you sit down with your Bible, or listen to a sermon or think about belief, remember that the whole thing is a soap or a sit-com, not to be taken literally. Your task is to journey to the heart of the language to find out what it really has to say about you and your world.

'But that's not what most vicars say about the faith on a Sunday morning!' True, but I'm afraid they're lying. You see, what I'm writing has been bread and butter Christian teaching for decades at university and colleges. Every priest knows this. Many priests understand and agree with this, but it's rather like the cabinet papers which are kept secret for thirty years: the big question is, when do you let the people know?

We're always reading in the Sunday papers the results of polls which tell us how many bishops don't believe in the virgin birth and a literal resurrection. The media try to suggest that it's strange and when a former Bishop of Durham was brave enough to speak publicly about what most priests know and talk about privately, there was uproar.

Most vicars opt for an easy life. They don't relish mutiny in the pews, complaints to the bishop and no cucumber sandwiches, so they feed the people what they want to hear. They stroke the teddy bears and adopt the language of the people. All at the nursery is peaceful. To themselves, they justify this great cover up: 'My flock aren't ready for this information yet, too young in faith, too fragile in spirit ... so much suffering ... unnecessary.' It's an invidious system of untruth which keeps the congregations locked up in a spiritual childhood.

9 THAT GUY CALLED JESUS

If only the tabloids could do an exposé on Jesus! What the headlines might be! The trouble is that the paparazzi weren't around then to catch him in compromising positions, neither were the tabloid sharks looking for a juicy bit of gossip or innuendo. Unfortunately, the truth about Jesus has been lost for ever and what we are left with is the highly biased writings of his closest friends and supporters. They were out to make a point, drive home a message, salvage a disaster and save their necks. They distribute what is clearly propaganda promoting their cause.

Don't misunderstand me. Parts of the biblical writings are beautiful and inspiring, but only safely so if we realise what we are reading and how it came about.

I enjoyed the part in the film *The Life of Brian* when Jesus loses his shoe accidentally on the way to the cross. His followers interpret it as a sign that from then on any would-be disciple must only wear one shoe!

There is so much rubbish talked about Jesus. He has been used as a coathanger to cover with all our own ideas, hang-ups and needs. For most churchgoers it's not a question of what Jesus thought or said, it's what they decide which matters.

WHAT CRAZY AND DAMAGING CLAIMS!

One of the worst things that comes up time and time again is the fact that people claim that Jesus was 'sinless'. They claim that he was God and that he was Man but that he never put a foot wrong or fouled up in any way.

You can see even the most intelligent people become blind when reading the Bible. In fact it's quite chilling, watching them ignore the facts in order to keep their own mistaken beliefs safe and intact.

Even in the Bible you can see that Jesus was far from this uncomplicated saintlike character floating through Palestine. Yes, he was inspiring, passionate, creative and perceptive (to name just some of his good points), but he was also temperamental, he made mistakes, was prejudiced, rude and offensive, insensitive, undiplomatic and thoughtless. As a child he did a bunk and went missing. When his distraught parents finally caught up with him, he showed no regret and answered their questions with cheek and insolence. I'm not sure whether Joseph and Mary punished him but he certainly deserved it.

In a later episode when he'd grown up and was surrounded by supporters, his mother and family come looking for him. Someone interrupted him with the news of their arrival but his reaction was cold and uncaring. As far as he was concerned everyone there was his family, so what was so special about his mother turning up? It was the sort of reaction that parents complain about today when their children get sucked into various cults and are brainwashed into cutting their family ties.

THE ROT GOES DEEPER

So many people cherish a rosy view of Jesus as 'gentle, meek and mild', but it doesn't take very long to shatter that illusion if you read the Bible.

At one point a distressed mother, quite beside herself with sorrow, comes to Jesus and begs him to heal her sick and dying daughter. Well, our stereotyped images of Jesus come flashing into view. We're sure that his heart was moved with compassion, that he only wanted to help, that he worked one of his many miracles, that Superman Jesus came to the rescue!

We're mistaken. Nothing of the sort. First, when he was told she had come, he was annoyed and wouldn't see her. She was kept outside and, worse, told to go away. But she wouldn't and her persistence annoyed the disciples who were embarrassed at all the fuss she was making.

In the end Jesus let her in and she poured out her heart to him. Jesus remained stony hearted and stony faced. 'No' is his reply. He can't and he won't help. The reason — because she comes from a different country and a different faith and the goodies in his sweetie bag are for the Jews only! To add insult to injury, he doesn't mince his words. He likens her to a dog at a party; the food is for the guests, not for an animal.

But she is some woman! She argues with Jesus that he may think of her as a dog, but even dogs at a party are given scraps to eat. Is he so ruthless that he won't throw a morsel down to help her daughter?

'My God!' you should be thinking, 'is this Jesus?' It sure is, I'm afraid — but on the other hand, actually, I'm not afraid.

BETTER WHAT'S REAL THAN A LIE

The Jesus of our fantasies is a worthless figure, holy, sinless, a plastic dummy of unreality. No one has ever met anyone like it. Those who pretend to be like it are so artificial and those who try to be like it spend their lives in torment crushed by their continual failures.

How many people do you know who live under the

shadow of guilt and self-recrimination because of their weaknesses and their mistakes? Throughout history the church has enjoyed spreading the message that Jesus was perfect and we are sinners because this puts us firmly in its power.

The church appears to hold the key to our freedom and our healing. In fact many churches peddle the pre-school version of Christianity which goes something like this. We are dirty sinners. Jesus is squeaky clean. On the cross Jesus was able by magic to take our dirtiness away and his dying and rising was like a big washing machine bringing us all up whiter than white. All we have to do now is wear the Jesus badge on our hearts and we're heaven bound.

And guess who gives out the badges? The church!

As far as I'm concerned it's the greatest con trick in history, and it's allowed the church to become the most powerful and wealthiest global multinational company today. The message plays upon people's fears and uncertainties, it gains access to their hearts and loyalties and it drains their pockets dry.

Yet it has so little if anything to do with Jesus.

PLEASE WILL THE ROGUE JESUS STEP FORWARD

Here is a real man, who is just like the rest of us. Mary and Joseph made love and he was conceived, like the rest of us. He was a good lad at times and a brat, too, who needed a clip round the ear!

He grew to be a man with fire in his belly, love in his heart, and a vision in his soul. He was a dreamer and a thinker, a poet and a philosopher. He discovered that love was more important than anything else, even where matters of religion were concerned, and that made him flexible and spontaneous in his contact with people.

But as with us all, it was a learning process. He made mistakes, judged things incorrectly and had his conclusions challenged, as by the woman above.

At times his emotions took over as with the well known episode in the temple when he was so angry at this holy place being turned into a corrupt market place that he just simply went berserk. He damaged the traders' property, whipped them violently, shouted abuse and threw them out. In today's world he would have ended up in court convicted of assault, criminal damage and disturbing the peace, and people reading the paper would have been going, 'Tut, tut!'

I like this man Jesus. He is useful. He is real. It would help perhaps if we changed his name and called him George or Wayne or some name which got rid of the layers of obsequious rubbish which the sound 'Jesus' conjures up for us.

Here is a man able to adapt, to change, to grow, able too to change events around him, even indeed the history of the world. Here is a special man whose life and memory live today giving so many good insights and great wisdom for us all.

In fact, his life had such an impact upon others that his followers gave him the highest and greatest accolade of all; they said that God had been with them, and they began to refer to him as the 'Son of God'.

THE INFECTION SPREADS

What people don't realise is just how dangerous words are and how the beliefs which spring from them mould the way we think and the way we behave. The innocent words 'Son of God' soon turned into a nightmare.

From Son of God he was elevated in their thinking to be God himself; as God he couldn't have sinned so he was declared 'sinless'. If he was 'sinless' he couldn't have been born in the normal way so Mary must have been a virgin.

If Mary had to be a virgin then something had to be wrong with sex.

If Jesus was perfect, male and unmarried then priests should be unmarried, male and perfect as well. In fact if anyone was to follow Jesus they had to strive to be perfect and after all, if he as a man could manage it, why couldn't we?

The whole thing had become derailed and was bound to bring disaster — and it has, to many lives.

10 SO WAS SHE A VIRGIN THEN? AND DOES MONEY GROW ON TREES?

Sunday Schools are dangerous places which should be regulated by a watchdog and parents warned of what happens. They are normally staffed by well meaning old ladies or hyped up evangelical converts who have one aim in mind and that is to brainwash the kids.

The children are taught that what the Bible says is true and that the stories really happened, even the miracles. They are exposed to a world of make believe which their teachers say is real and not fantasy.

If children question the party line they are made to feel unfaithful and points about doubting Thomas are made and that God is really pleased with those who believe in Jesus without needing to see him.

If one steps back and looks at the process, it's either a laugh or a form of intellectual abuse. The children are brought up in a world blessed with the scientific advances which have changed the course of our lives. But religion has been kept in the cupboard with a weekly dusting by the faithful. It's a world where women get pregnant without sex, where men float on clouds and angels pop round to visit; where dead people climb out of their coffins and water changes to wine; it's a world where snakes talk, the lame walk and money for your tax turns up inside a fish!

As an allegory, like Tolkien's *Lord of the Rings,* this is fine. But if your teachers are hell bent on making you believe it's all true, then we've entered the mad zone.

C. S. Lewis's books about Narnia are bestsellers; children love them, but they don't spend their time banging on the back of their wardrobes in hope!

STAR TREKKERS

I know that those who get involved in special interest clubs like the Elvis Presley Fan Club or the Star Wars following or the 'to boldly go' brigade, sometimes go somewhat wacky, develop crazy ideas and act and live as though the whole thing were true, but apart from their most nutty followers, if pressed, most can own up to the game they are playing.

Not so the religio-nuts. They have a glint in their eye and a glazed look on their face and for them it's you who are off beam for not believing in their wild and magical biblical merry-go-round.

THOSE POOR KIDS

Imagine sane people choosing to send their children to the Moonies or some strange cult to be taught about religion.

They wouldn't. But these same people wouldn't think twice before sending them up the road to Sunday School. In their mind it's a whole different set up. Let me warn you that it isn't, and what happens to the poor children when they go, is far from being helped to enjoy the treasures of the Bible, they are given a version of believing that they will discard at puberty as being childish and irrelevant.

FOR A START LET'S CHANGE THE NAME

As with the name of Jesus, so with the word 'Bible', it's a turn off. It carries too many ghosts and too much of a stigma. Perhaps *The Eastern Collection* would be better, or *Dreams and Poems*. We need to get rid of its image.

Then the church has placed a clever security cordon around the Bible, by calling it 'God's word'. If people dare to question it, or rather how the church interprets it, they are being disrespectful to God. It's hard to process the guilt that it creates and it keeps most people quiet.

But let's cut through the flannel and see the Bible for what it is. They are not God's words because God didn't sit down and write them, human beings did. If you want to understand how the Bible came about then go into any bookshop and look at the array of books on the shelves and the papers at the counter. We have to tell stories about our lives, set our imaginations free and reflect upon our experiences.

Of course some authors are better than others and each year we watch the round of award ceremonies. It was at an earlier award ceremony that a group of believers made various nominations. The categories included best lyrics for songs, best poem about the earth's formation, best account of Jesus' life etc. The winners had their writings put into a collection called 'The Bible' for general reading, something like having some of the Booker prize winners put into a single volume.

That is such an innocent process and it is such fun to read through all the entries and express our opinions.

'What a beautiful story!'

'That one leaves me cold.'

'What rubbish!'

'Yes — that's powerful.'

THE TORTOISE INSTINCT

You only have to look around you to see how much people resemble tortoises. It's the hibernating instinct. Everyone finds a nice cosy way of life full of the things they always do and the places they always go. They climb into their little boxes where everything is the same and they feel safe. It's a way of sleeping your way through life!

Change is the monster to be avoided. Luckily, in every-day life things are advancing so rapidly that people's boxes keep getting knocked over or destroyed altogether.

Not so with the church or with its Bible. It's a clever ploy. Convince vulnerable people whose worlds are being turned upside down that there is one place that always remains the same and one manual that is never out of date and you're onto a winner.

I can remember seeing the posters at the youth club: 'Jesus Christ, the same yesterday, today and for ever'. It felt comforting but on closer inspection it was meaning-less.

You only have to look at the books written a hundred years ago to realise that the writers lived in a different world. Of course there are similarities with our day but so much of what they knew and how they felt is alien to us.

It's true that Jesus said some wise and challenging things which resonate with us and are useful for us. He also came out with some rubbish which rose from his experience but which needs to be binned by us.

That is the healthy and proper relationship we should have with the Bible. We should be setting about its pages as a miner digging for diamonds — confident enough to discard the waste and preserve what's valuable. But this is in stark contrast with the dreamy-eyed Bible basher for whom every word drops straight from God's lips and nothing can be set aside. For them there is no distinction between rock and diamond.

THE NUTTY AND
THE CRACKED

We don't have to look very far for proof that much of the Bible should find its way to the trash can. In the Old Testament there are horrific tales of the mass slaughter of people because God got the hump or wanted their land; people being stoned because they had dared to collect wood on the equivalent of our Sunday; women who were thought of as dirty for a week if they gave birth to a son and for two weeks if it was a daughter; gays and mediums who were to be put to death, and a ban on anyone with any defect from becoming a priest. God certainly wasn't politically correct. There were to be no wheelchairs at the altar!

In religion, watch out for the wrigglers. They are the people who have an answer for everything. They know that God is going to heal their friend's cancer because the church is saying prayers. Their friend dies. The sane person concludes that God flunked on this occasion, or that this simplistic approach to prayer is flawed. Not the wriggler; for them God's healing came in the form of death — they've been rescued into heaven!

It's hard to argue with people like that. When you confront them with the sticky passages from the Old Testament they either claim that God's ways are beyond ours or they say that it's the New Testament that is for us today.

THE STICKY TRAIL
CONTINUES

It doesn't take long flicking through the New Testament to find more purple passages. Jesus tells people to gouge out their eyes if they can't stop ogling pretty women; supports the barbaric practice of cutting off the hands of thieves; tries to stop a man from going to his father's funeral and teaches that the bad will be burnt alive.

Later on God strikes two new converts dead for stealing, Paul warns that gossips, the arrogant and boastful, those who disobey their parents and the gays and the lesbians all deserve death; he teaches that God has put every government in place and we must obey them (even Hitler's!) and that people shouldn't marry unless they can't control their sex drive!

We're told that Jesus will whisk the faithful up into the clouds when he comes again, that God will trick the people who don't believe into doing wrong and so have an excuse for destroying them and that the world as we know it will end with the coming of beasts and dragons.

Now anyone who can accept that lot must need help. The terrifying truth is that many people are taught by the church that they must. It's like taking a dreaded medicine: they are encouraged to hold their nose, close their eyes and swallow hard, the difference being that this is poison to their intellects and to their souls.

THE GREAT SIEVE AND
DAZZLING DIAMONDS

There is a very sensible alternative to this hocus pocus. Everyday people wrote down their ideas and reflections about life. You only have to look at how children's views differ from their parents' and how each generation comes up with new ways of doing things. Add to that the astonishing advances made in science and technology and you can see how thought develops in leaps and bounds.

Someone writing 8000 years ago certainly had different ideas from someone writing 2000 or 4000 or 8000 years later! So the reader of the Bible has a fascinating task of watching people's ideas about God changing.

They find the early writers describing God as someone who was jealous, angry, vengeful, unjust and unmerciful and then the later writers correcting that description to God being someone who was more tender, loving and compassionate. In fact, as the great mystics of faith have tried to help us realise, all spiritual writing is a record not primarily about God but about ourselves and how we understand our world and our lives.

Having taken a great sieve and shaken hard to remove the prejudiced, inaccurate, wild and primitive muck, there before you remain jewels of considerable value.

11 TREASURE

Having mentioned some of the muck, it would be good to become Aladdins and open the treasure chest and pick up handfuls of goodies.

The brightest and most perfect parts of the Bible are those which speak about love. They say that if we are to have a healthy way of describing God then it must be in terms of love – so much so that wherever you find love you have stumbled across God. They expose the religio-nuts who Bible bash and point the finger, with telling remarks that anyone who doesn't love those they live with, can't claim to love or even know God!

The writers tell us that if we love each other then God lives in us and his love is made complete and perfect in us: no talk about church attendance, confession, doctrines or the like, just the simple and healing practice of loving.

But this loving is not the sickly sweet Hollywood variety, it has teeth. It's a love that feeds the poor and helps those in need, that visits prisoners and tends the sick; it's a love seen in action and not just heard in fine words.

God is described as being patient with us and as caring for us; someone to whom we can turn, who will share our problems and our pain.

Such talk about God is a way of pointing us towards a way of living together based on the practice of love. It's a way of life in which we try and sort out our own messes and problems and support others while they do the same for us, but where no one accuses, judges or condemns another. Indeed such love should flow between us that we could even tell each other about our weaknesses with confidence.

We are encouraged to stand up to evil and to bear the cost of doing so with dignity and grace; to be self-disciplined and to hold on to all that is lovely and good.

Love must always come first, blossoming in patience, kindness, gentleness and most tellingly in the offering of forgiveness. We are set high goals in terms of striving after truth; but again not the skin-deep variety which is about keeping our noses clean, much more the penetrating truth of being able to know and work with what is, in all its raw reality. This is me; this is the situation, warts and all.

PURE GOLD

The writers lead us to realise that immense power lies

within us; that our inner reserves of hope and courage and joy run deep if only we would spend time in finding them, in fact so much so that there is nothing too difficult for us to overcome.

They speak of discovering a place of inner peace which is pure contentment, in which each and every need has been supplied, every desire fulfilled, every longing satisfied, where all is calm, all is complete.

A key is to learn how to love oneself, for how could we ever love another person whom we don't know, if we can't love the one person we really do know!

SCATTERED NUGGETS

Working our way through the Old Testament can be some task and there's not much reward as lorry loads of waste get taken away. However, there are special parts. With a little imagination and editing the stories can be retold in an exciting way, especially for the kids.

Surely every child should know about Noah's Ark, the Tower of Babel, Joseph's coat of many colours, the ten plagues, the parting of the Red Sea, Balaam's donkey, the Golden Calf, the fall of Jericho, Samson and Delilah, Samuel hearing God's voice, David and Goliath, David and Bathsheba, King Solomon, Elijah and the prophets of Baal, the sufferings of Job and Jonah and the whale, to mention just a few.

Likewise every adult should know about and have read the Psalms, the love poetry of the Song of Songs, the wisdom of Ecclesiastes and the words of the great prophets like Isaiah, Amos and Hosea.

SELECT, SIEVE AND
BE SENSATIONAL!

Some of you may be thinking, 'But I don't want to tell my children about some half crazed God who drowns everyone or screws up people's lives like Job's just for the hell of it.'

Fair enough! I agree; and that's why people should have the confidence to read the Bible selectively, editing out the hairy parts and explaining what's left so that it makes sense and its point is heard.

Don't suggest to the children that Jonah was actually swallowed by a whale or that Balaam's donkey actually spoke or that God actually flooded the whole earth. No, rather tell the story with enthusiasm and fun and then begin to speak with your children about the invisible world of which they are already well aware.

Talk to them about the hidden voice of conscience that tells Balaam off, pictured in the donkey speaking, and the dark, consuming and dangerous place we find ourselves in if we practise evil, very much like the stomach of a whale. Talk to them about the way we can find ourselves at odds with the whole world with everything going wrong when we live selfishly, very much as if we were hit by a disaster like a flood.

The explanation is the key to unlocking the treasures of the stories. If a child can go away thinking that God is the sort of God who would wipe out thousands as a punishment or would send great monsters to swallow us — this is to make the stories banal and stupid, and yet that is what happens in most Sunday Schools, even from most pulpits, week by week.

LET'S TRAP GOD!

But the laugh is that those who claim to be most faithful in believing in God often do so out of insecurity and fear. Their ideas about God end up by being so frightening to them that they have to gain control in some way.

The Bible becomes a type of cage in which they think God is caught. 'This is God's word,' they say. 'We can understand everything about God's will for us; all we have to do is obey!' What they are in fact saying is that if we can reduce God to words in a book and if we can hold that book in our hands and speak about it and explain it, we achieve a useful shift of power and focus away from God to ourselves.

They really mean, 'It's us you must listen to, be taught by, follow and obey. Our interpretation, explanation and way of doing things is right.'

They end up being God!

SURPRISE, SURPRISE!

The God of the Bible is a God found everywhere and not exclusively anywhere. So the adventure to create a clearer picture of God involves a humility which is constantly being surprised at where God pops up next.

Devout Christians shouldn't be surprised if atheists know God better than they do, or drug addicts better than the archbishop, or a Muslim better than their priest. Don't be shocked when God speaks to you more powerfully through the *Sun* than the Bible, or through *EastEnders* rather than *Songs of Praise*, or through walking over mountains rather than a church service.

That's why those Christians who think that the main way they'll grow in their knowledge of God is by sitting in church are very much mistaken. It's one of the last places that you're likely to discover God.

Go out into the world. Read widely, including the Bible and other spiritual works, but also anything and everything. Live fully, have open arms towards those you meet, listen to their opinions, ideas and insights, don't be afraid of life and what it offers and within the energetic nature of all this rich and varied experience, if you are looking, and if you desire to see, will grow a spiritual awareness and a sense of God.

God's word is a living conversation spoken in the interweaving of all our lives.

12 BELIEFS THAT MAKE SENSE

The approach I have taken towards the Bible should be our approach too towards what the church teaches.

Throughout the world people remain bowed down under mountains of guilt and live in fear of God's anger. They worry in case their actions offend God and hope they are carving out a safe niche in heaven. Jokes abound about the gates of heaven and the fires of hell and people build their whole lives around trying to do 'what's right'.

One cruel teaching has been the Roman Catholic crusade against condoms and contraception, but it doesn't end there. You only have to listen to a judgmental *Thought for the Day* on the radio or visit a local church to cringe at the views being expressed. My heart goes out to all those whom I can feel being crushed by judgment and condemnation, whose sense of identity is being ridiculed and who are being quite clearly put on the scrap heap by the church.

Whenever you come across a church teaching that makes no sense and cripples your life then scrap it. Wear a condom and stay on top!

VAMPIRES AND
CANNIBALS

One of the beliefs that has bedevilled the church up to this day involves the bread and wine of communion.

In many church services they share out some bread and wine. It's a simple and lovely symbol of a family sharing a meal together while they remember loved ones past and present, especially Jesus who started the idea.

But then the religio-nuts take over and contaminate this lovely act with their crazy theories and philosophies. For them the bread and the wine actually become Jesus' flesh and his blood. Not only is this a distasteful form of cannibalism but it also messes up the beauty of what the meal was meant to achieve. Instead of it encouraging love and understanding it has created some of the fiercest arguments throughout church history and has separated husband from wife and set communities at war with each other. It's an example of belief running wild with terrible consequences. Here's to those who hold their own communion services or who take communion whether they are baptised or not, whether they are Catholic, Anglican or whatever. Here's to those who break through the barricades erected by the church and sit down happily to eat together.

THE SACRAMENT OF
PIE AND MASH

What people don't realise is that beliefs are not valuable or real in themselves, but find their value in directing our attention to the importance of something which is real and everyday.

Some people walk away starry eyed from communion saying they have met with their Lord, yet would never invite anyone to their homes to eat with them, certainly not a stranger or someone in need. At communion they are on a personal ego trip, a spiritual orgasm.

If people really wanted to experience communion they should want to invite their neighbours round for a meal, then the local street dwellers, the Jews from the synagogue, ex-offenders from the rehab unit, even their enemies. This is communion; not the artificial, stereotyped and clinical farce that happens weekly in most churches.

The most intense experiences of communion I have experienced were receiving *prasad* in a Sikh temple, sharing food at a Jewish Passover meal, being given biscuits on a train by a Czechoslovakian family, being invited to share a ball of lentil paste with a beggar in Calcutta and eating a Macdonalds with a tramp in Croydon!

PASSING THE BUCK

Prayer is another example. If you have ever listened to the prayers in church or on radio you'll perhaps have had the same sickening feeling. Every week it's 'Dear God, we pray for the poor that they may have food; for those whose legs have been blown apart by land mines that they may be healed; for the unemployed that they may find work, for prisoners that they may be helped.'

It's a shopping list of doom and woes. Those who prepare the prayers and some Christians seem to gain a sadistic pleasure from wallowing in suffering, as though in some macho way they are proving that however ghastly things are, nothing will knock their faith and trust.

The people who have prayed in this way so often have done a clever dumping job. Here are the problems, we've mentioned them, you sort them out! When they leave church they have no intention of giving *their* money to the poor or challenging unjust trading practices. Campaigns against land mines are not for them. The local unemployed project is written off as the work of loony lefties and they wouldn't go near a prison if you paid them!

MEANINGLESS

Prayer like this is meaningless and it achieves nothing except self-deceit. That is not to say that prayer, when properly practised, isn't helpful.

Prayer at best is a means of focusing on areas of concern both personally and in the world generally. It's a means of growing in empathy, identifying the potential for change and for progress. It's understanding if we have a part to play in affecting the issue, mustering and unlocking inner resources for our action and feeding upon the reserves of hope and beauty and healing which lie beyond us. As such it is an energising, enthusing and enabling experience, very different from the great opt-out clause in most church services.

THIS HEAVEN AND HELL
FIASCO

Let's call a spade a spade. No one knows what happens when we die. That is a fact. So when there is talk about heaven and hell and life after death we are not moving in the corridors of science.

However, if someone you love dies then it is impossible for you to believe that they have gone; the sheer stupidity and cruelty of death makes us angry. How dare God or anyone take our beloved away. It's an outrage.

It's not surprising that we want to fill the dark loneliness with words and images that will bring comfort, answer questions and heal the pain. We are quick to reach for the Paracatemol. Heaven is a good painkiller.

But just as so many commit suicide using Paracetamol, so the heaven solution can be deadly. You often hear people express a hope that they are going to heaven, and the church has often chided people to behave well to make sure of a pass through the pearly gates.

But the result, as with much of religion, is to deaden

the conscience and produce moral lightweights. It's the consumer society all over. Play your cards right, save up enough spiritual points and what a bonanza – heaven awaits you! The incentive for keeping to the straight and narrow is a reward, like the system of loyalty cards which the major supermarket stores have issued.

The most devastating result of this can be heard when Christians smugly say to one another, 'Well, this life isn't what it's all about, I'm banking on what's to come!' What a tragedy to miss out on so much of life if only to find out that when the coffin lid falls, that's it!

BRINGING HEAVEN DOWN TO EARTH

So let's make sense of the language. People, unless they have been born with some disorder or have been damaged along life's way, have a sense of right and wrong. They are also aware that doing wrong screws you up, whereas trying to do good leads to fulfilment and happiness.

Around the world, in our own neighbourhoods and in our lives, there are endless examples of heavenly and hellish situations brought about by the people involved or by circumstances out of their control.

Our job is to push back the frontiers of hell and to spread the experience of heaven. We want to create a world where wars don't rage, where people can eat, where disease is overcome, where happiness is widespread, where people are understood, accepted and loved.

SO WHAT ABOUT THE HEAVEN UPSTAIRS?

The honest answer is that while we can always hope, we do not know if there is a heaven. Nevertheless we need the language of poetry and of pictures to help us express the bonds of love which forever tie us to those we love, even beyond death. They remain alive for us in our hearts and in spirit. We dream of them, feel them and smell them. They influence our thinking and our choosing and we are never free of their presence. The language of heaven gives us a home in which they can live, a place of beauty warmer and more true to their involvement with us than the soil of the grave.

But if we press the pictures and demand that they hold scientific truths for us, that there is actually a place called heaven, and Sue or Brian are actually walking around there, then we create more problems than we can solve and we reduce the Impressionists' art to ridicule.

13   PANCAKES AND PASSION

Another regular hassle is Lent, when everyone is told by the church to give up something. Chocolate, beer, sex all come a cropper in the desire of the faithful to please God by their sacrifice!

Again, though, it's a cosmetic job and it misses the point. The story of Jesus struggling in the desert is not anything to do with chocolate, bed clothes or Hammer House of Horror devils trying to trick him into a pyrotechnic display of miraculous magic. Nor is it an

American-style drama featuring the latest hunk as Jesus, the underdog, caught in a titanic struggle between good and evil and managing to come home all flags waving, having championed the world.

It's about the ordinary and everyday struggles that you and I face throughout our lives. It's about whether to queue jump, be held back in our job by helping a colleague, make vulgar signs to the next driver, support a campaign working with the poor or spread a bad word about someone. It's about whether to go on and on buying more things for ourselves, do voluntary work, spend all our time in the pub or golf club, bear a grudge against people, or deliberately cause harm to someone.

It's about whether to gazump someone, take drugs, sell your story, stab someone in the back, help an enemy in need, have an abortion, take someone to court, divorce, sell a dodgy car.

TURNING UP THE HEAT

All of us face thousands of choices throughout our lives. The religio-nuts would want us believe that it's all a straightforward battle between God and the Devil, that the Bible gives us all the answers and that choosing is simple.

These same people often come a cropper, because life isn't like that and such an approach produces either artificial puppets or a nervous breakdown. The frightening truth with which we are faced is that there aren't easy right and wrong pathways. While there may be common factors and trends, nearly every decision is unique and every set of factors different.

The image of the forty days Jesus spent in the desert trying to make up his mind is about the heat he experienced, the endless time and the loneliness involved in choice.

The whole charade of giving up petty things sells us very

short indeed. In fact when I hear Christians joking about what they are going to give up this year, I realise that for them it's an easier option to keep Lent at the sweetshop level than to enter the desert of personal choice.

TONGUES
(AND NOT FROM THE
BUTCHER'S SHOP!)

Beware those church groups that put on a spiritual razza-matazz. Their services are pepped up, their flock are all on a type of spiritual drug and what happens is a cross between a rave and a seance. At first sight people speaking an unknown language, called 'tongues', may be rather thrilling to the newcomer. It may also be a complete turn off! However, if it attracts, watch out. Things aren't all that they seem.

Such groups regularly claim that God is more fully present in their church than in other churches, that his Spirit is available to fill the lives of those who ask and that once filled they will be able to experience all sorts of things. For instance, they should be able to speak in tongues, or speak a message directly from God, or perform miracles. A whole cupboard-full of tricks are produced and can appear quite convincing.

SAFE IN THE
RIGHT HANDS

The cupboard's contents are quite fun and can be of help but they all should come with an instruction leaflet warning of the dangers of misuse. In most churches of this kind there is no such leaflet and the church officials make use of the cupboard for their own ends.

This 'gift of tongues' really sets people shivering. They are told that God will give them a whole new language, that strange sounds will come out of their mouths, that they only have to try and the language will flow. It all sounds rather creepy and odd. In fact it's a perfectly normal earthly process and nothing to be afraid about at all. Language is made up of different sounds. Some sounds form words, others sighs or tones. If you experiment, anyone can enjoy the fun of making different sounds with their mouths and vocal chords and begin to produce a pattern which takes the shape of a new language.

I remember as a child developing a wonderful array of sounds which I would speak to the other foreign children on holiday as though I was speaking another language. It was great fun. In the end the sounds become familiar and, as with any language, can sound beautiful or rough.

WHY NOT JUST TALK ENGLISH?

The idea of using tongues is that words require thought and thought often gets in the way of being able to relax or express the feelings inside you. Perhaps you are really angry, distressed out of your mind, worried sick, on Cloud Nine, or whatever; we are not all poets or writers and our words can let us down, but sound can say it all.

In the same way that listening to a song can grate because the words may not fit our mood, listening to some instrumental or classical music can carry our emotions and give vent to our longings. Tongues give us an orchestra to play out our innermost senses.

Tongues can be beautiful when used privately and when they are used with others, either spoken or sung, but when one person uses them in a church it brings us to the next trick.

PROPHET AND PROFIT

No sooner has the tongue finished than the prophet is rolled on — the one whose gift it is to interpret the sounds that have been heard. Someone in the church will stand up and begin speaking as though they were God or Jesus. 'I am pleased with my people ...' The rest listen and receive God's message. Many are overawed at the idea that God is actually speaking to them.

Let's come down to earth. God hasn't done any such thing. Sarah or Tim has the sort of personality, intellect, creative mind or imagination to be able to capture the mood of the community, express its feeling or be perceptive about what will be the next challenge it might have to face.

Sometimes what they say is right on, sometimes completely off beam. Those who hear it as God's words and swallow the lot are to be pitied, particularly if they're being told to give all their money to the church! The wise need not be threatened by the process because they can sift out the rubbish and learn from the useful.

DENIALS AND ACCUSATIONS

Of course those involved are so brainwashed that they could never agree with this approach. They will provide a thousand justifications, proofs, personal testimonies and evidence by the bucket load to show that it's all miraculous.

The strange thing, however, is that by so doing they somehow rob people of the beauty of what's actually happening. Learning about using tongues may be as helpful to Edith as yoga is to Bob. Growing in confidence to be able to speak a word from God may be as fulfilling for Andy as painting a picture is for Charlotte.

The contents of the cupboard are available to anyone. They don't require any special status, any miraculous experience, any special prayer or extraordinary happenings. They are as miraculous as learning to walk, talk, write, draw, sing, act, swim or any of life's amazing array of opportunities for self-expression.

AS IF ONCE WAS NOT ENOUGH

So what's all this second coming business with Jesus coming back for the great day of judgment and bringing the world to an end as we know it?

It's *Independence Day* stuff, the bread and butter of sci-fi fans and the like, but it has no meaning for us if you take it at face value.

By now perhaps you are getting into the swing of this approach and can do your own interpretation. Lets scrap the toddler's version of clouds and fire and brimstone and look for the heart and thrust of the story.

All of us are capable of constructive interpretation, but to get you started, the belief is meant to make us feel as though we'd just heard that a very special and dear friend would be coming to visit after a long time away. It makes us remember past experiences, take stock of what news there is to share, make practical preparations, wonder what the friend will make of us and think of us now, indeed everything begins to be taken up with the knowledge and awareness of the possible visit.

In the case of imagining that Jesus was the friend, the feelings might take on a sharper focus, as though the visitor was also our teacher and moral guardian all rolled into one, as though in a way the visitor was our own conscience.

Believing in the second coming is nothing to do with some future 'end of the world' drama. It's about whether we live our lives and make our choices in such a way that should a good and holy conscience pay us a surprise visit, then our hearts wouldn't go a-racing because of what we had to hide.

14 MADAME TUSSAUD'S

I'm not sure whether people assess their level of fame by whether they have been immortalised in wax. Some say it's hard to tell who's false and who's real in Madame Tussaud's, that people begin to strike up a conversation with their pop idol or revered politician and find them particularly dumb!

The church is brimming over with wax. Not only are so many of the people wax look-alikes, posing and posturing as Goody Two Shoes, but also the way they believe has turned what's true and what's false upside down. Prayer meetings, holy communion, church services, Christmas, Easter and Whit Sunday — these things aren't real. At best they are rather lovely games that we enjoy, works of art that we love or plays that we perform together. The task of a painting or a poem is to present life while not itself being life; and that is the task of religion too.

The danger, however, is that churchgoers become so caught up with their religion that it's as though they had become obsessed with art and are unable to leave the art gallery. For them the real world is an unwelcome distraction. They adore an Impressionist's landscape but despise the real countryside. They see *Phantom of the Opera* 20 times but have no time for the disabled. They become consumed in Mills and Boon but can't make a relationship work. They say that they love God but haven't the time of day to give to anyone around them.

MELTDOWN

Sometimes it's necessary to turn the heating up and light the fires until the dummies have slowly gone.

I used to infuriate certain members of my church by suggesting that they regarded themselves as devout and faithful believers but that they hadn't a clue what their beliefs meant and that their believing was thus a waste of time.

They would go red in the face and their hearts would race as they declared, 'But I believe in the Crucifixion and Resurrection and that Jesus was the Son of God and that he healed the blind, cured the lame and in the end that he ascended into heaven in front of everyone.'

These were the same people who were incapable of working with difficult situations, unable to offer forgiveness to others, unaware of how to find hope in despair. They were uninterested in helping people see their way through problems or helping to get someone back on their feet. Their beliefs were all words and talk, convenient cushions with which to buttress the invading world, a pleasure park of contrived forms of speech which provide a thrill here and there but send you out into the world empty-handed.

UNPACKING WORSHIP

Church services can be either horrifically dull or top entertainment, but whichever form they take they are meaningless unless you understand what's going on.

For a start let's cut God out of the picture. Although the people involved may want to boost their own egos by thinking they are putting on a dazzling circus spectacular for God, the truth is that the whole show has nothing to do with God at all.

A church service is a group of people choosing to put together a programme of words, music and actions which carry meaning for them. The question someone attending should ask is: What is the meaning?

It can be fun to sing together; it is special to enjoy beautiful words being read, particularly if those words are wise or instructive; it can also help us to think together of common concerns. All these things happen naturally in worship. There is nothing mysterious about it. You find similar ingredients in concert halls, theatres or poetry evenings.

Then there are the more intriguing parts of the service. We are invited to confess our sins, to seek forgiveness, to offer praise to God, to declare our beliefs and to receive bread and wine. These appear rather religious but on closer inspection they too are very ordinary.

The idea is to encourage people to be self-critical, to desire improvement, to learn to be grateful, to express what makes them tick and to be willing to sit down and eat together with friend and enemy alike.

They are the raw ingredients for happy, healthy living together and in a church service they take this stylised form.

BUT YOU CAN'T BE A CHRISTIAN IF YOU DON'T GO TO CHURCH

How often have we heard that said? It's rubbish! As I've tried to show there are some who do the stylised bit perfectly, the hymn-singing, communion-taking brigade, but they are some of the most unpleasant human beings in the real world.

In contrast, there are some who wouldn't be seen dead in a church but they know their faults, try hard, love life, protect their wisdom and have time for and would share their last penny with anyone. These are the true Christians, the genuine believers.

If it's ever a choice between religion and reality, between church and conscience, between liturgy and love, choose reality, conscience and love every time. If asked to burn the Bible, renounce your faith and put the sacrament of bread and wine down the toilet, do it, if it means protecting someone. There is nothing in religion or about God which is ever worth causing damage to yourself or to your family or to others; if you think there is, something's gone wrong with your thinking or with those around you, and you need to get help.

PITY THE SUICIDE BOMBERS AND THEIR VICTIMS

The world is full of people doing terrible things for God. They cut off people's limbs, blow up buses laden with passengers, gas commuters, gun down children, torture prisoners, knee-cap victims, slaughter and hijack.

The young strap bombs to their bodies and drive their lorries towards checkpoints, they plant bombs in their luggage and board an aircraft. In the inferno that results their bodies along with many others are obliterated. Why? For God and for dreams of heaven. Oh, how much the priests, the holy men and the spiritual writers of the past and the present have to answer for!

Such wild and crazy actions may seem a long way from home, but that is only because we have tamed the hairier sides of our religion and made it fairly respectable. Beware, though, the potential terrorist bomber with whom you shared tea this morning or beer this evening.

It may have been the sweet lady or jovial chap who slips into the conversation that God has told them to change job, move house, go to church more often or give up gambling. So far so good, but tomorrow it may be to reject their parents, disown their child or break a lifetime's friendship. It's the same mentality that leads people to maim their opponents and kill their enemies.

Once we start believing that God is telling us to do things, no one knows where it may lead.

NOT AT MY
PARISH CHURCH

So many parents watch unperturbed as their children innocently trip up to church for the youth club or a uniformed service. Localised religion seems so harmless in this country, and often it is. The only deaths or danger to health occur out of boredom.

However, there is an upsurge of Bible bashing, hand waving, happy clappy worship, miracles and wonder-centred Christianity, and many of the local churches have been affected. What is even more dangerous is that as these same churches get their acts together and present themselves with a glossy freshness, so they appear more consumer-friendly and modern than others.

People come away thinking that all is well at St Swithin's and isn't the new vicar lovely. But what they need to find out is what the vicar and the churchgoers believe. Underneath the glitz and the glamour can be a deadly and ruthless belief system which could seriously threaten you and your family's health.

THE SAFEST AND BEST

If you are one of those people who has a belief tucked deep down within you, who is quite comfortable in saying a prayer now and then as the need arises, who quite likes popping into church at Christmas and Harvest and who intends to try and live in a Christian way, then to you I would want to raise a toast. You are the safest and the best form of Christian I've met. Don't let anyone knock your faith or make you question your status as believers. You are as much a part of the church as any churchgoer is, and God loves you just the way you are.

You keep the true faith alive and well and preserve it from the zany, the fanatics and the over-the-top brigade, as well as from the dour, the stalwarts and the stick-in-the-muds. You are the salt of the earth, the gentle light that pervades our world.

PART THREE
A PERSONAL JOURNEY

15   IT STARTED WITH A KISS

I was one of the 'safest and best' type of Christians until I left school at 17. Involvement in a holiday play scheme for poor youngsters introduced me to Marjorie, a lovely young woman actively involved in the local church youth club.

She arranged my induction into prayer breakfasts and the strange new world of being a 'committed Christian'. Instead of reading Law at university I changed to Theology and set my heart on becoming a priest.

I was caught up with Bible-believing Christianity and

the idea that there were simple answers to guide me through the great unknown adult world was certainly attractive. At university I was drawn to a happy clappy 'spirit filled' church which was all the rage at the time. Its spontaneity and belief in present day miracles were music to the student mind convinced that everything was possible. The fact that with young fervour and utter dedication, significant things were achieved over these years, only lent force to the sense that God was working powerfully.

THE GHASTLY TRUTH

One thing troubled me, though. I couldn't understand how Christians could live extravagantly and speak about the gospel of love while the poor were starving. I became the college 'prophet' decrying the waste and wantonness of the bar, discos and the great yearly ball. You can imagine just how popular I was!

I became consumed with the desire to ensure that my life expressed my beliefs and so everything 'unnecessary' to life was discarded. I slept on the floor, ate simply and washed in cold water! Any surplus money I had was given to charity.

As well as those personal rigours, I also moved bureaucratic mountains in setting up a shop, marketing goods from the poorer countries, which still trades from the college. Then having graduated, I felt compelled to travel out to Calcutta to work with Mother Theresa's Missionaries of Charity.

This was to have a profound influence upon me. After working with a group smuggling Bibles, medicines and other materials into eastern Europe in false-bottomed suitcases and specially adapted cars, I hitchhiked my way to India.

I was picked up by car thieves in Turkey, tear gassed in Iran in the riots which preceded the revolution and ended up being taken to my accommodation in Afghanistan at gunpoint! Nothing, though, prepared me for Calcutta. The squalor and horrific poverty I found there shocked me.

For most of that year I worked in the slums of the city, washing, cooking and living beside the people in their struggle for survival. I saw appalling sights of self-inflicted deformity, beggars with large parts of their bodies openly rotting. I saw murder and violence in the pursuit of food and money and the darkness and ugliness of poverty.

Through all of this I realised that the Bible-believing, happy clappy approach to Christianity and to faith generally was severely lacking and that I needed to let go of this comfort rag approach.

POINTLESS PRAYERS, PRAYERFUL PRACTICE

Calcutta has a cathedral where each Sunday the rich and the well-to-do file in to say their prayers and chin wag outside, while chauffeurs watch their cars and the sun makes their elaborate saris sparkle.

I was sickened at how easy it was to take any set of words, even Jesus' unequivocal ones about wealth, and manage to twist them so they lost their meaning. I was sickened when I arranged for a poor man from the slums to be given Bible lessons at a Biblical Study Centre and he was thrown out because his clothes were shabby.

In the end I had less and less to do with the churches and their artificial services and poured all my energy into trying to help those in need. My happiest moments were being able to save the lives of a young woman and an eight-year-old boy who were dying on the streets. When I left I was able to invest £14,000 which I had raised in England, so that the interest could help fund a hospital for women suffering from tuberculosis.

SAGE AND GRASSES

Over the next five years my thinking changed dramatically, not least through a chance opportunity I took to meet with hundreds of people from other faiths at a great assembly in Kenya organised by the World Conference on Religion and Peace. There were American Indians burning grasses, Buddhist monks who had been 'given' to the temple as children and Jain followers who wouldn't walk on country paths for fear of treading on an insect.

I was voted on to the executive committee and travelled widely to their subsequent meetings. It was a new world where there were nearly as many different approaches to faith as there were faces present.

Yet there were common factors also. I would hear a Muslim, a Christian, a Baha'i, a Brahma kumari and a Jew all say with confidence and sincerity that their truth was the 'real' truth, their way the 'right' way, the words of their holy book or prophet or whatever was the 'correct revelation'. They were like children saying with conviction, 'But mine is best,' or like parents speaking proudly of their children, villagers of their village, citizens of their country, teachers of their school or employees of their company.

At its most innocent, it was the rather lovely loyalty we all show to what is ours. At its worst it was the raging bigotry which causes wars and justifies terrorism.

LOVE VERSUS BELIEF

Having served as a Church of England minister for three years I then took up a job in the South working with a priest called Brian. He was a chaotic and complicated man who needed to feel he was loved, but out of his insecurities came a deep love for others. He had little time for religio-speak, philosophical argument, church routine or the stuffed shirts of the hierarchy. People always came first.

I remember writing a highly controversial article about the local workers at the armaments factory having 'blood on their hands'. Brian agreed with the arguments I presented but his overriding concern was for Sid who worked at the factory. He had to earn a crust for his family and the article wasn't going to change anything other than make Sid's already difficult life more difficult.

THE WORLD ON A BUS

During my time with Brian I arranged for 50 young people from different countries, faiths and philosophies to travel together on a journey from London to Moscow. As well as seeking to forge links between east and west, the itinerary included visits to Auschwitz, Bergen-Belsen and other sites of significance across Europe.

As I spent more time with people from such widely different backgrounds it was apparent that love created a true and safe community.

THE AMAZINGLY WONDERFUL GIFT OF YOU AND ME

There is nothing more wonderful in this world than people. They are an exquisite combination of everything that has been given to them and everything that has happened to them; how they have responded and what is ingeniously, creatively, uniquely theirs.

I became aware that if I was to be allowed to journey through the defences into people's inner world then I had to want to and be willing to love them from start to finish. I had to accept them, treasure them and cherish them, never pointing the finger and never judging, but understanding and reverencing the holiness of the other person's world.

I realised, too, that such love is very rare.

DON'T CALL ME VICAR!

By the time I became a vicar I was well and truly down the path of thinking that our ideas, values and beliefs are as arbitrary as the families and countries we were born into. There is no mystery to it, just an international lottery of chance as to where we emerge and what we end up thinking.

It becomes rather sickening then to be surrounded by people who think that the only place to live is England, the only colour skin to have is white, the only faith to have is Christian, the only denomination to be is Church of England and the only approach to faith is their own.

In fact, what being Church of England, Christian, white and British meant was as irrelevant as being bothered to find out the name of the new priest.

'Morning, Vicar! Morning, Vicar! Morning, Vicar!' I could have been a cardboard cut-out, I don't think they would have noticed. 'Don't call me vicar, please,' I used to say. 'My name is Jonathan.'

NOT QUITE THE TRADITIONAL

My approach was very much that faith was to be fun and a church was for everyone, not just the cliquey members; power and jobs should be shared round.

This ruffled feathers! It had been a world where the vicar did everything, where his word was a command, where a tight system of rule and precedent operated and where all knew their pecking order.

We had to move from a dying, irrelevant community to being a vibrant and modern place buzzing with energy and life.

16 NOTHING'S IMPOSSIBLE

There was so much that needed to be done and the only realistic mandate for change would come from the people. As the diehards held power on the church council I arranged a series of monthly new committees to which anyone could come, new or old, to voice their opinions.

These became the powerhouses for change. New ideas flowed rich and fast. Decisions that might have taken years ordinarily were made in months: new services, music, groups, outings were set up, children were welcomed, chairs cleared, carpet laid and toys provided in the church for toddlers during the services as well as nappies and crèche facilities. The stranglehold that the select few had exercised over the church for decades was broken. Everyone was involved in the revolution that took place and as the church became a more friendly, outward-looking place so people began to flow in.

When I arrived, ten people came to the main morning service, 75 overall on a Sunday, and the church income was £21,000. During my five years there as vicar, at its height there were on average 254 attending with income having risen to £77,000. Christmas, Harvest and other special services saw the church overflowing, with on one occasion nearly 500 people coming.

THE BUILDING WAS FALLING DOWN

For nearly 20 years the congregation had watched as the church slowly subsided; they despaired and offered each other gloomy predictions that nothing could be done.

They hoped that I would help repair the building but instead I helped them to see the problem as a marvellous opportunity to transform an old fashioned church into a multipurpose building serving the community.

We raised nearly a quarter of a million pounds and today the church is equipped with facilities which are the envy of most parishes around.

ZEST AND ZING

I love taking services in a meaningful way and I can't stand the pompous, stiff and churchy way that most vicars meander through the words. I wanted Sundays to sparkle and so they did.

Adults and children enjoyed coming. I gave the children and adults communion if they wanted it whether they were confirmed or not; I could never understand how Christians could share a 'meal' together and leave some people out.

At Easter a local donkey helped in the worship and at another time we packed our animal service with creatures of all kinds! Easter Sunday was great fun, with eggs hidden all round the church and pandemonium breaking out when the signal was given for the search.

On Whit Sunday we released hundreds of orange, red and yellow helium-filled balloons as a sign of the fire of the Holy Spirit carrying messages of love across the world. At Christmas the whole church would be ablaze with hundreds of candles as we sang 'Silent Night'.

There was always something happening. For Comic Relief we had a special comic service in memory of St Rudolf the red-nosed reindeer; on April Fool's Day one year, I arranged for local fire officers to interrupt the service and empty the church for a fire drill practice supposedly ordered by the Council; on another I distributed green Communion wine instead of red.

THE CENTRAL MESSAGE

I was always careful to preach a message of love and acceptance. A community could only survive if there was a basic understanding that everyone was struggling to make sense of their lives. One person's way may not be another's but the family of the church was there to offer support, care and unconditional love and never to point the finger.

If mistakes were made or things went wrong, the simple truth of the Christian faith assured us that there was nothing love couldn't face and that with forgiveness and understanding a way could be found through everything.

No one was to be rejected. No one's views were to be ignored. No one was ever to be pushed away. It didn't matter what they believed, thought or did. People were to have a sense that they were accepted unconditionally into the heart of the church and nothing would ever change that acceptance of them.

LIKE BEES TO A
HONEY POT

As the message spread, so the church family grew to accommodate all sorts of people. There were lots of your 'ordinaries', but there were also many whom you wouldn't normally find in a church. A woman with a serious weight problem, a man whose kids had been taken away; people from a local residential unit who used to call out unpredictably in the services, alcoholics . . .

Whenever anyone came who had special needs I would try and ensure that we provided whatever was necessary. A loop system for the hard of hearing, Braille books for the partially sighted, wheelchair ramps and toilets for the differently abled.

If poor people came to the church we would help. Accommodation was arranged, clothes given, transport provided, visits set up. Everyone was regarded as special, unique, to be loved and cherished. If it was possible, I tried to give jobs to and involve those who perhaps otherwise would have been sidelined.

AWARE

We certainly didn't have our heads in the sand. During the ambulance strike I arranged for the bishop to come and we stood with the strikers around their makeshift fire. The ambulance station was virtually next to the church.

I was shocked during the Gulf war when I heard that the bishops had approved the heavy bombing of the Iraqi conscripts. I decided to imitate the biblical story, in the book of Daniel, of the divine finger that wrote a warning on the king's wall.

I planned to be arrested and to try and capture the media's interest in the strength of opposition to the random bombing. In the end I took the case on appeal up to the High Court and was commended by the judges for my sincerity and integrity.

Each October we tried to draw attention to the plight of the poor and homeless and built a shanty town outside the church. We lived in it over the weekend and on the Sunday, instead of wearing the normal embroidered priest's robes, I would wear some sacking and give communion with unwashed weathered hands.

However, middle class suburban Barnehurst was not

used to its vicar being arrested or offering communion as a down and out look-alike!

THE BLOSSOMING

People were encouraged to have ideas and follow them through. Banners were made, a music group began, songs were written, people were trained in pastoral care, a marriage preparation course began. We hosted an international conference of world peace makers, sent a member of the congregation out to India, donated thousands to good causes. Everyone's talents were welcomed and used.

THE BACKLASH

But while this amazing and wonderful growth was happening, there were the 'mutterers and the murmurers'. These people were of the old school and their noses had been put out of joint by the influx of new faces and the loss of their power, as well as by my fresh approach to faith and life as a Christian.

What I wasn't expecting, and I realise now I was naïve in not understanding this, was the way that people could be unaware of the real reason for their difficult feelings and hide them behind an apparently more worthy cause.

For instance, someone whom I had appointed to a post of responsibility became resentful when I spoke with him about a personal problem with which he was struggling. On the surface he remained sweetness and light but behind the scenes he wrote letters to the bishop complaining about my preaching.

IN THE FIRING LINE

As a figurehead and leader I became, as any vicar, the focus for many people's private thoughts and fantasies.

When people came to me, it was hard to decode whether they were being genuine or devious and whether even they themselves understood what was going on inside them.

I remember being mystified as to why one woman had become so angry with me over a period of months. When I asked her she came up with a list of criticisms justifying her anger. However weeks later she admitted that she was having sexual fantasies about me and would I please go to bed with her. I declined the offer.

There was the woman who related to me as the son she had never had, a man the lover he had always craved, another the father for whom she had longed. I was none of these things but trying to dodge the mistakenly felt emotions that then came my way from these people was very hard.

SUFFOCATING

From the start I had resisted all the pressure upon me to become a 'puppet vicar', doing and saying all the things that were expected of me. However, with time this became increasingly hard.

With conspiracies hatching fast between one of the churchwardens and the church readers about my faith, my writing and my preaching, I felt that there was a desire to muzzle me. I was loved as long as I kept my views to myself.

There was a small but vociferous group who didn't like the children in services, who thought it was wrong to hold social events on a Sunday or have alcohol at church functions, who thought the Bible should be taught as though it were fact.

I became very unhappy. I loved my work and was proud of building a community where people felt loved and included, but I hated the hypocrisy of those who were more than happy for me to accept them, but who were not willing to accept me unless I conformed.

I felt I was slowly dying. The person I was and the things that I believed were bursting to come out, but I wasn't allowed to be honest or real. I shared this openly with my staff team, but the schemers merely saw it as another chance to reinforce their criticism of me. For them I was losing or had lost my faith. A suggestion was put forward that I be sent to a theological library to try and 'correct' my thinking!

17 COME THE DARKNESS

I discussed with my friends whether there might be a different way of working as a priest rather than being constrained within a denomination like the Church of England, but of course nothing had ever been tried along these lines. Anyway I was married, my career was tied up in the church, my house, pension and income all went with the job; it would have been a vast step to take and my wife would certainly not have been keen.

However, such thoughts became lost in the years of personal turbulence which followed. My marriage had always been stormy and complex. For many years we had managed the wounds which both of us brought to the relationship and amidst the difficulties enjoyed many rich and intimate moments together. From our love came our two children, who will always be the most precious part of my life.

However, over the years of conflict we grew apart. My wife gave herself to her career as a social worker and I sank myself into my parish work and we spent less and less time together.

KEEPING BOUNDARIES

As I've written, a priest becomes the subject of so many people's fantasies. You are someone's father, son, husband, lover, friend, teacher.

All the while you are on your toes and alert, it's possible to try and defend yourself against this onslaught, but if your own life is at a low ebb and you are lonely then it's very easy to believe in and respond to someone if they are offering friendship and kindness.

I had maintained professional boundaries for eight years, but my own personal circumstances had led me to a place of intense loneliness. I felt a stranger within my church and within my own home and offers of friendship appeared to be the only thing which had meaning in an increasingly meaningless world.

INVASION

During these months I found it increasingly hard to manage the pressures put upon me by the people around me. I became confused and somewhat lost. An older man in the church kept telling me how much he loved me and, to my discomfort, would come up and embrace me, then kiss me on the cheek in the vestry.

As in most churches, so many of the congregation were women that it was hard to escape them. One woman came and said that she had fallen in love with me and had gone for counselling. Other women came and expressed concern that I was looking unhappy and, claiming that their motives were entirely innocent, assured me that it was safe to confide in them.

Women invited me for coffee, gave me gifts, sent me surprise cards, letters, called round and incessantly phoned up. It was a barrage of inappropriate behaviour that I recognised for what it was and tried to keep at arm's length, but it sent me spiralling into turmoil and an even greater sense of isolation.

WATER IN THE DESERT

It was during these years I had two affairs. If I knew then what I have learned since, I might have been able to see and choose things differently. Yet it is a fatuous thought, because my understanding arises from those experiences.

Then, the friendship, love and tenderness offered was as water to a thirsty man. I felt as if I had no power or ability to hold back the intense feelings which flooded my life and no wisdom or maturity strong enough to protect me from what happened.

On each occasion innocent friendship became the path to falling in love. Then it was so hard to know how to harness or channel the energy which came from the passionate and intense experiences which followed.

THE TORTURED ROAD

I believe that no one can understand what a person's circumstances or choices are other than the person concerned. So many glib and abusive criticisms fly around in communities and most of them are far from the mark.

I remember vividly the moment I realised I was in love the first time; I was overtaken with a sense of dread. I asked my wife for help; it wasn't something I wanted or felt I had chosen. It was something which had happened and I thrashed round desperately for help to try and find a way out.

In fact the help that came, as so often in religious circles, tried to make everything tidy again by stopping the relationship but ignoring the reasons why the situation had arisen in the first place. Fairly typically, I fell in love again.

These were years of catastrophe. Looking back, and after counselling, I can begin to make sense of it all and of myself, but at the time I found myself drowning in a vast sea of experience.

NO SCAPEGOAT

I won't take the easy way out of blaming my upbringing, my genes or other people. I've always thought blame was an irrelevance anyway. My consuming passion is to understand. From understanding comes an informed regret which can find creative expression. I know that everything I have ever done, be it good or bad, has been something I chose to do, not lightly, but after considerable and heart-searching thought.

At the root of why I made the choices I did lies the answers to the mystery of myself. If someone truly loves you, it is that mystery they are committed to cherishing. So often, though, the word 'love' becomes a rod to beat you into silence and deceit.

The greatest love there can ever be is where one person says, 'This is who I am, what I am, what I think and what I feel. This is the unravelling and uncovering of my life. This is me.' And the other person says 'It is *that* you, in your raw honesty and entire nakedness, that I love and cherish. You can give me no more beautiful gift than the honesty about yourself.'

THE SEARING HEAT

But such love requires a marvellous and remarkable commitment. Such love will know the heights of joy and security and the depths of pain and terror. There is no more exposed place than truth and most of us both run for shelter ourselves and urge others to come in from the heat.

However, it is such love that is at the heart of nourishing relationships and healthy community. It affords people the grace to know and own themselves. From such knowledge comes the chance to grow towards the light and to cherish those who have remained by their side.

At this time of personal crisis I found it hard to find anyone who was willing to live in the light of such truth. People wanted quick, neat solutions, an automatic system to superficially apportion blame and trigger apology or to 'bin' the problem.

A GRACEFUL END

My wife and I separated in March 1993 and became involved in protracted legal proceedings concerning the care of our children. I chose to resign from my position as vicar and left the church on September 12th. My final service was packed with over 300 people and I was showered with gifts and with letters of appreciation.

I had achieved a well planned exit, for which the church authorities were grateful. However, the truth was very different from the appearance.

THE ATOMIC EXPLOSION

Lift off the lid and the community had become like a bowl of maggots writhing in scheming, plot and counter plot. The vicar's breakdown and custody battle was a marvellous opportunity to inject some spice into otherwise boring lives, to vent grievances and frustrations, to settle old scores and put the knife in. People took sides and plans were made.

The bishop, the churchwardens and some of my staff were informed about the two affairs. Letters of complaint were written to the church authorities and the gossip spread round the parish. Malicious and untruthful rumours were triggered — that I was gay, a wife beater, a pimp and dangerous.

The old traditionalists seized the chance to point the finger at the young women in the church, calling them inaccurately 'the vicar's harem'. This was laughable as the last thing I have ever been is a womaniser. Apparently they didn't object to the women of the Mothers' Union. They were over 70 and past it, true, but more to the point they were safe because they just wanted everything done 'as it's always been done'.

Meanwhile, evangelical officials in the diocese licked their lips at the chance to down this liberal priest whose faith had been a thorn in their side.

The church institution chooses repeatedly to welcome and make space for the good and 'respectable' in a person but in contrast to ditch their vulnerable and confused areas. In doing so, they jettison the fertile ground of a person's becoming and so rob the church of the reality of new life, growth and hope — in a word, of resurrection.

18 THE PLACE OF CRUCIFIXION

After years of personal torment, months of extreme pressure and so many painful events, I was in a traumatised condition. I felt aggrieved, particularly with one of my wife's friends who I believed had schemed against me during the custody proceedings and who had thrown wine over me at a church function.

My friends referred to her as the 'shit stirrer' and in my brokenness I had the idea of putting a sealed plastic bag containing dog muck and a wooden spoon through her letter box. Someone asked me once afterwards, 'But why did you do it, Jonathan, when you knew that she would have your scalp for it?' But, when you are lost and broken, you lose your power to think in this way. Against all the hypocrisy of the church desperately trying to keep its nose clean and of parishioners pretending to be super-saints, it seemed to have an honest and stark realism about it.

NO COMPASSION

It had been the bishop's plan to license me to work in another church in the autumn, and so during the summer

I had moved into a new house with my children. Now he realised that all the events within and surrounding the breakdown of my marriage had been so traumatic that I needed time to restore myself and he said that he wouldn't license me to the new job. I should have a break, take time to heal and then consider a return to church work.

The priest responsible for my house arrived the next day and told me that I had four weeks at the most to get out. I remember begging him as a Christian and as a human being to give me time to find a new home. He refused. My words to him set myself a new direction.

'Michael, if this church has room for you but not for me and my children, then it's not Jesus' church and I'm glad not to be working with you.'

DEVASTATION

Over the course of those months I had lost my marriage, my family, my home, my income, my job, my community, my reputation, my colleagues and many of my friends.

I lay in bed for one whole day, paralysed with the immensity of what had taken place. It was a place of darkness, fear, insecurity and despair. I couldn't condemn myself for my choices, because I knew that, while they may not have been 'right', I had always done the only thing I felt I could have done at that particular moment.

It was naïve to imagine that the worst was over. The intrigue and scheming continued. There were more custody battles with tens of thousands of pounds being wasted on legal fees. There were leaks to the press of sensitive and personal information designed to embarrass me and my friends and I was plagued with malicious phone calls, mail and forms of harassment which were fascinating in their ingenuity and at times pornographic and abusive in their content.

I had often thought to myself when besieged by doting

parishioners that it was all a farce. I would sometimes pose the awkward question from the pulpit, 'If the Nazis had invaded England I wonder which of us would have collaborated with them, which of us would have betrayed our neighbours and our friends?'

WHEN THE CHIPS ARE DOWN

It is an uncomfortable thought. It's easy enough to smile and laugh when everything in the garden's rosy, but I wanted to shout out to everyone, 'But would you still be sickly sweet? Would you drool over my every word? Would you still love me if your cardboard cut-out vicar moved one day and said, "Hey there, I'm here, I'm human and I need help!"?'

Perhaps that sense of the fickleness of everyone's friendship fuelled the fire of what happened. I accept that my 'Hey there' was quite a striking one, but not unusually so. They had always known I wasn't your everyday kind of vicar; it could have been anticipated that my difficulties would be as marked as my successes. But people were only happy if the sky was blue.

I was turned from a saint to a monster overnight. It has always amazed me how so called 'Christian' groups can do this to a person. It has happened to many priests and bishops. The media go and interview parishioners who say such banal things as 'We thought he was such a nice man; we really looked up to him, he was always so kind. But now we see he's wicked, disgusting, evil, darkly motivated, an abuser, a hypocrite.'

The critical words pour out as blood from a slashed artery. This is indeed a battle to the death. The cardboard cut-out priest has dared to come to life and burst the bubble of people's fantasies; he must be stopped at all costs. The knives come out. He's far better dead than alive, for dead men don't speak!

SENT TO COVENTRY

I became an outcast. The fact that Jesus suggested that the work of the 'church' was to seek out, find and help the outcast and the lost was inconvenient. Instead the new job description adopted by the church is to create a cosy and exclusive club for members only!

In the years that followed my leaving in 1993, almost without exception no one from the church visited or contacted me; calls I made to former colleagues were not returned, visits I made were spurned, letters ignored.

It was ironic that early on there was a knock on the door. Two middle aged women were standing outside. 'We're from your local church,' they said, unaware of who I was. 'It would be lovely if you wanted to come to any of our services. We always give everyone a warm welcome.' I desperately wanted to say, 'Well, why has your priest just thrown me and my children on to the street then?'

SURVIVAL

I began to realise that my personal survival was at stake. I had offended a system of religion, and they were wanting to carry out as effective a smear campaign and dumping job as they could — just as a great multinational might have reacted.

In the process they used the muscle of a large organisation. Officials were sent into the parishes, secret letters were circulated and the 'old boy' network snapped into operation. Off-the-record telephone conversations, parish magazine articles and church announcements were all directed at destroying my integrity.

Throughout I offered to meet with those responsible to look at what had led to the unhappy situation and to find a way towards reconciliation or, if that was impossible, at least towards conciliation. But that wasn't the game that was being played. Christian language became redundant. Forgiveness, renewal, hope, resurrection were fine in books and services but not for real life.

HOLY WEEK EXPOSED

I had always thought the week leading up to Easter was important and each year I had put an increasing amount of thought into it. We recreated the drama of the last days of Jesus' life. Special services were arranged and imaginatively presented.

On Maundy Thursday I held a service as near as possible to what Jesus might have shared with his friends. Then I would stay up all through the night in the church and encourage others to accompany Jesus through his last night of trial and torment. During the evening hours the church was stripped bare. The chairs, carpet, church furniture, everything was removed. By Good Friday the only thing that remained was a vast crude wooden cross. It was a day when I encouraged everyone to eat no food and to spend most of the day in church in prayer. When Jesus was supposed to have died, at 3 p.m., I extinguished the candle beside the cross and lay prostrate upon the floor as a sign of the total darkness which had consumed us all. It was a journey into evil, despair, hopelessness and nothingness, a journey into a place where even God had been killed and was no more, where we had done our worst deed. At that point there could be no words, only the silence at what we had done.

Then the Saturday saw feverish activity. The church had to be cleaned from top to bottom, the furniture polished and returned and then the church filled with the most spectacular and extravagant displays of flowers. In the evening everyone crawled into their beds exhausted and knowing that they were to be up at 4 or 5 in the morning before the dawn. Easter Sunday was the most important day of the year. I encouraged people to make the effort and come to the early service. At its peak about 100 came one year.

CHRISTIANS LOOK SO GLUM

People often think of the church as a place filled with long, sad faces, as though Christians enjoy wallowing in suffering. That wasn't going to happen in my church! True, we had journeyed into the place of suffering, but we were going to enjoy just as much of the opposite.

Our celebrations would go on for as many days as Lent. Easter Sunday was the kick start. Everyone would be asked to come silently and gather outside the church. Those involved in the service would creep into the church to put their robes on and make their way in the darkness to the church door.

Outside, a bonfire would be crackling furiously. The service is to mark the resurrection and is all about the life, light and joy of Jesus that even death cannot destroy. At a certain point in the service the people would shout out, 'Christ is risen indeed. Alleluia. Alleluia. Alleluia.' Then every light in the church would be switched on simultaneously and the organ would crash in with every note possible.

The children's mouths would drop open and the adults would be mesmerised. The church looked breathtaking, flowers rising from every shelf and ledge available, the priest's vestments covered in sparkling cloth of gold, the silver and brass gleaming and everyone's faces beaming with surprise and wonder. After the service we poured into the church hall next door for a cooked breakfast and to enjoy the rising sun of the new day pouring in through the windows.

BUT WHAT'S THE POINT
OF IT ALL?

One year one of the congregation came up to me and asked why I made such a fuss of Holy Week. For them it all seemed rather pointless. It happened to Jesus long ago, so why were we play-acting it all again?

'Because,' I said, 'It's one of the central insights of our faith that we all so often face crucifixion and that we can rise again.'

In those last troubled years, though, I became aware that for many church people it was just a form of play-acting that had no link to their lives, and that they would no more be able to rise again than they would be willing to be crucified.

19 RESURRECTION

My fears were fully justified. In the furnace of human difficulties into which we plummeted as a community in 1993, our Holy Week experiences counted for nothing. The services had become ends in themselves instead of pointing people to a better way of life.

So, as I lay on my bed during that long painful day, I knew that we had all experienced a crucifixion. I was responsible, but not only me, everyone who had been involved had had opportunities to help and heal or to stir and scheme. We had nudged each other along the corridors of evil.

It was the place that we symbolically visited each Good Friday, so we should not have been strangers there. We needed a wise and graceful person to come and rescue us, to intervene and restore us. But the bishop, the archdeacon and the church officials involved were all either inadequate in knowing how to cope or were spiritual lightweights.

SAVED BY MY BELIEFS

Holy Week had taught me that there is always a way out; that disaster can be a doorway to opportunity; that one's worst nightmares can be faced; that even in a place where everything hopeful has been obliterated there is still hope; that you can be stripped of everything and have nothing, even lose your life itself and still find new life beyond the nothingness.

I knew that I was at a personal Good Friday. I knew I had to make the following period of time my Holy Saturday and pour all my energy into preparing for a new life and that in good time I would celebrate a true, real-life Easter Day when my life and the lives of others would be restored. Lying in bed wasn't going to solve anything. That was exactly what my opponents wanted me to do. Coming back to life was the last thing they expected.

MIRACLES HAPPEN

The next day I went out to find a house. The estate agent asked, 'And how are you going to pay, sir?'

I had no money and it wouldn't have been possible to arrange a mortgage. Surprisingly, I replied, 'Cash.' Somehow I had to believe that if I had enough faith and if I was doing everything in my power to sort things out, then this mountainous problem could be overcome.

No sooner had my friends heard that I was in dire straits and had to find the money than they came forward with offers of loans which covered the amount.

In two weeks I was the freeholder of the property and proudly holding the keys! I had also secured a job with a finance company and had begun their training programme. It had been essential for me to find the kind of employment which gave me the flexibility to look after the children and this was perfect.

REAL FRIENDS

A few people were astonished at how the 'friends' dropped off once I had left the church. As a vicar I had at one time received as many as 350 Christmas cards; these were down now to a handful. But that handful were so precious, because my real friends were those who accepted and loved the real me.

It was a whole new experience to know that, when someone smiled at me, it was genuine through and through. We shared some intensely moving times decorating, packing and unpacking, and all the things involved with moving in.

We ate meals on the floor, then progressed onto boxes and finally to the table as it emerged from the chaos. We were a church together. All our things were in common, we shared our money and resources; our meals were our communion and our prayers were expressed in the practical commitment we gave to one another.

REAL FAITH, REAL ME

I didn't go near a church during this time, nor did I open the Bible or ever say a prayer. I was sickened by the outward forms of religion that had been shown to be so bankrupt of meaning. I still believed as passionately as I did before but my faith was now expressed solely in my everyday approach to life.

As the weeks passed I was aware that I was becoming happier and more carefree. I was able to own myself and love myself. It was liberating not to have the dark shadow of the Church breathing down my neck and suggesting I wasn't the right shape, personality, character or style of believer.

I was doing well and being appreciated in my new work and I devoted myself completely to my children, who have always been the most important part of my life.

TWO GOLDEN YEARS

It was an astonishing time. There were treasured moments with the children, beautiful holidays with friends and daily a sense of being restored and a growth in confidence. By the summer of 1994 I knew that I could no longer deny my role as a priest.

The great question remained whether I should arrange to see the bishop and ask for an appointment within the Church of England. The thought made me claustrophobic. I had escaped a system which had been slowly strangling the life out of me; it would be sheer madness to go back into it. Here was a chance for me to create a new pattern of priestly work in this country working independently of any denomination. My friends were enthralled by the idea, if a little apprehensive, and encouraged me to go for it.

YOU CAN'T MAKE IT
ALONE

It's hard to throw off that sense of inner fear. The explorer and pioneer have no idea whether their expedition or project is going to work. It was a high risk situation. A new career had to be created from scratch, but I knew that it was right.

I spent chunks of time alone, thinking and planning. Times beside the river under the vast sky, soaring sea birds and endless stretches of water were particularly inspiring. Using traditional Christian language, I would say that I knew God was calling me to this new work and that he would use me in it to spread a message of love and acceptance. But such words so often get in the way. What I did, anyone can do. If you create space for yourself, dare to be alone, open yourself to the creative powers of nature, then your thoughts will galvanise themselves and decisions flow. This is the real meaning of prayer and God guiding you.

THE BROCHURE

The most important part of my launching a new career was how I was going to describe myself and my work. All of this had to form part of a brochure in which I gave a description of myself.

This was so important. It was the chance for me to stand up to all my anonymous critics who had whispered and muttered about me behind my back and to reject the smear campaign carried out by the Church of England. The real Jonathan Blake could stand forward and introduce himself.

I launched the brochure on my birthday in the October of 1994. Although I knew it would be of interest to the media, I hadn't quite been expecting the reaction it caused. For the next few weeks chaos truly reigned. There were articles in most of the nationals, endless radio interviews, appearances on television news and current affairs programmes; the phone was hot!

It proved to be a wonderful launch. The initial flurry of activity gave way to more serious appraisal and articles appeared in the *Guardian* and a full-page feature in the *Independent* describing me as 'Britain's first freelance vicar'. I rather liked that; I knew the Church of England wouldn't!

CUTTING THE TIES

I was a priest within the Church of England. The greatest amount of soul searching I had to do was whether I should sever my links with this one denomination in order to be truly independent.

It was a frightening prospect, like cutting an umbilical cord, but if I believed that I was on the right road I had to believe it would work out.

It was a significant and symbolic moment when I chose to effect my Deed of Relinquishment and thus give up my office as a minister within the Church of England. In my own mind I had signed away the chains of a compromised earthly system of religion which had for so long restricted my ministry. I had taken myself out of its jurisdiction and control.

I no longer needed to gain a dubious authority from an institution which I believed was corrupt. A calling to the priesthood comes from God and is recognised by the church. When a person has had his calling recognised and has been ordained as a priest, he retains the character of his priesthood for ever. The law makes it clear that no one on earth can remove it.

This is true even if a cleric has been defrocked. However, I had not been defrocked, nor removed from office; nor had my licence been taken from me. I was a priest within the Church of England who had taken time out to restore his life after the breakdown of his marriage. Now restored, I had made a choice not to exercise my priesthood within that denomination any more.

I was free at last to be fully God's priest and to show the true love of God to every person, whatever they believed, whoever they were, wherever they came from — the love which is about acceptance, forgiveness and respect.

The Church of England was taken by surprise.

KNEE JERK

It was hilarious. The first reaction of the Church of England was to phone up the lawyers to see how they could stop me. After all, I was going to make Christian ministry available once again to the everyday person. That wasn't allowed. The new system operating today is that vicars will only help the select few who jump through various hoops or who are regular churchgoers. The rest hardly get a look in!

The Church of England wants to force people into its buildings to maintain its power base in each community and to continue to milk the parishioners financially. My new ministry would cut right across that form of narrow-minded protectionism and could undermine the Church's prestige. And what if I was just the first?

It wasn't long before they discovered that I had pulled the rug from under their feet. I was no longer within their system or under their authority. I was a free spirit — a bit like Jesus and the disciples, answerable to the people and to God. There was nothing above board that they could do, only put more energy into the dirty tricks campaign to make things difficult for me.

BACKLASH

I wasn't surprised when it came, but it was distressing nonetheless. The most ugly action taken was by a group of clergy who anonymously contacted a tabloid Sunday paper and a local paper to 'dish the dirt'. 'Did you know that he had affairs?' they asked. The journalist who emerged from the shadows one Friday night to interview me seemed to have more sympathy with me than with them, but the exposé was inevitably uncomfortable.

I knew I had to take the rough with the smooth and so I became resigned to the reality that journalists often misrepresent and distort the truth for their own ends.

However, once the cycle of crucifixion and resurrection is in the soul and the blood stream, you can cope with anything.

PART FOUR
THE NEW HAS COME

20 A PRIEST FOR THE PEOPLE

'We've both been divorced ten times, we have 28 children between us, we realise now we're lesbians and it's really important to us to get married upside down in a swimming pool. Can you help?' Well, I haven't quite had them that unusual, but some come near!

The most beautiful part of my ministry is when people have come to me with their tails between their legs, anxious and often wounded at having been rejected by umpteen other priests. They tell me their story and ask if I can help. To speak the words, 'Yes, of course I can!' is such a privilege.

I have seen people visibly grow in stature and in

confidence before me. I have had people break down in tears of relief. I have seen smiles blossom across barren faces.

CLERICAL ABUSE

I can't begin to write down all the horror stories I've come across during my new work. They leave me speechless.

There was the couple who had asked the local vicar to marry them. As the man had been divorced the vicar asked them to come to see him every week for an hour for six months, at the end of which he'd decide. Guess what? At the end the vicar said, 'No.'

There was the single mum whose baby had a rare terminal disorder. She was beside herself when she came to me because her vicar had said the baptism had to take place in the main morning service. Her child had very special needs and a public service would have been totally impossible.

There was the family whose first three children all went to Sunday School and for whom faith had an important place in their lives. The children's baptism certificates and candles were all proudly displayed in the sitting room cabinet. But their vicar had refused to baptise their fourth child because the parents didn't go to church enough.

POWER HUNGRY

The trouble is that many vicars are 'little' people who enjoy their sense of power. They gain some sort of thrill in thinking they can play God and judge between the so-called good and the bad, and have people come to them with bowed heads and a grovelling manner.

At times, when people approach me their voices are apologetic and soft; they've been reduced in some way by contact with an institution which has found them to be lacking and which has regarded them as too inferior to merit a marriage or a baptism.

If only they could realise that there is little difference between their local vicar and a tin pot dictator; that there is probably more Christian understanding and practice in their little finger than in the one who has just roughed them up.

THE SUNSHINE OF ACCEPTANCE

I was determined that at the heart of my new work would be a thoroughgoing acceptance of people — a warm-hearted, non-judgmental, open-armed approach to the whims and ways of any I met. Some people have looked concerned: 'But is there anything you wouldn't do, anything that would shock you?'

Well, if so, I haven't discovered it yet. True, people come with a wild array of ideas which at times appear wacky and weird, but in every case there has been a reason why their request has made sense to them and had meaning in the context of their lives. If I encounter things which at first sight are uncomfortable to me, I regard them as a challenge and try and work my way into the shoes of the people concerned and to understand why it is valuable for them. In this way I learn from journeying with them to whole new worlds and cultures.

TRUTH

I believe that truth is a precious gift to offer one another. But truth is not a one way gift. There has to be an environment in which truth can emerge and grow.

There is no greater killer than condemnation. It drives people within themselves. I have had so many couples say to me, 'We weren't sure whether we would tell you the truth, but . . .' Vicars who take a heavy-handed judgmental approach are fools because they prevent people from being able to be open and honest with them.

If people know that they will be accepted whatever they have to tell, and that you will give them the dignity and respect of believing in their right and ability to work out their own lives, then they will offer you the gift of their inner selves.

REACHING OUT TO THE THOUSANDS

In the first four years of my new ministry I have taken services which over 40,000 people have attended. Unlike a church, these are not the same tight-knit clique week in and week out, but different people becoming involved in an act of worship.

What is even more significant is that many of the 40,000 would not have experienced Christian ministry had my work not existed.

It was pitiful that while I remained within the Church of England the 'Decade of Evangelism' was under way — ten years of outreach to those 'outside' the Church. The Church formed numerous new committees to organise events, thousands of pounds were spent and hours of work went into thinking up new gimmicks to attract the 'floating non-believer'.

At the same time priests during my training would look out to other countries and wonder enviously at the wave of new life sweeping the churches abroad. In addition, bold new initiatives were being taken by many communities forming their own cluster groups of believers and moving away from the more stereotyped churches.

So many colleagues were depressed at the moribund nature of the churches' life in the United Kingdom. Discussions began, 'If only . . .'

What has been ironic and marvellous is that my

approach to ministry has turned out to be 'frontline evangelism' (to use dreadful jargon) and has released the energy and sparkle experienced by churches abroad.

NO DEVIOUS PLOTS AND
PLANS

I always found the scheming behind evangelism distasteful. Christians would be sitting together pooling their ideas about how to entice some husband, colleague, young person or whoever into the church. There may be an invitation to the church social, a guest service, special prayer meetings or a dinner at home. People would swap their in-house tricks and boast of the scalps they had won along the way.

The religio-nuts would have a mental score card and would be on the watch to check out whether the preacher socked the gospel message home properly, or whether the new convert managed to bring the chatter round to Jesus effectively enough.

The beautiful part of my new ministry is that there are no such tactics, no ulterior motive or hidden agenda. I am naturally fulfilling my priestly vocation to love. By so doing, countless opportunities to 'evangelise' present themselves.

Not that I have any intention of changing anyone's thoughts, beliefs or mind. I have an intention to love and I believe that love, unconditionally given, has its own divine power and energy to fulfil God's design.

THE CHURCH AS IT WAS
MEANT TO BE

As I drive around the country, I pass innumerable church buildings. Most of them are locked, forbidding kinds of places. They are held in the grip of a few zealous followers who often have devoted their lives to them.

They have the same passionate loyalty to 'their' church as others do to 'their' pub, football homeground, or country. They hold the reins of power and all hell breaks out if it is threatened. And so the churches remain no-go areas to most people.

It is thrilling, then, to be giving back to the people what has been stolen from them by the institutionalised Church. Suddenly, a private garden, a front room, the local pub, a nearby hotel, a country estate, a motor cruiser, a mountain top become the church 'building'. My vestry is a child's bedroom, a pub cellar, an outcrop of rock, an apple orchard.

This approach to ministry mirrors how Jesus and the disciples spoke, preached and took services, in the homes and on the hilltops of the Holy Land. It stands in as sharp a contrast to the over-regulated Church of England as the Jesus brigade was to the Judaism of its day.

21 CRYING OUT FOR MINISTRY

In the first four years of my new work I have seen the trickle of interest become a flood. There is no need for a clever advertising campaign or any gimmicks. People are crying out for this approach to ministry. All they need to know is where it's available.

In the first few months I was glad if I had on average two enquiries a week; now that can be as many as 90. Over the four years, despite a slow start, over 4000 people have contacted me for information, and at the present rate that will only increase. Over 40,000 have attended my services as guests. I have travelled as far afield as Ireland, Crete, Minorca and Morocco. I have covered over 130,000 miles in Great Britain, visiting Scotland, Wales and all the coasts. I have visited hundreds of parishes and countless dioceses. I have conducted weddings, baptisms, namings and blessings, funerals, communion services, ministry to the bereaved and other counselling, exorcism, blessing of homes and rings, anniversaries, the renewal of wedding vows and ministry to pets.

I have baptised over 650 people. *And the church had dared to call these people 'non-Christians'!*

Every family, couple and individual that I have met has had one thing in common: a sincere and meaningful faith. Their desire to express important moments in their lives in a spiritual manner arises out of their own inner awareness and appreciation of the things of faith.

True, it's not necessarily a neat, well packaged and glossy form of believing, but then it's all the more genuine for not being so. Unlike the 'factory produced' Christians who can bleat the answers but often haven't understood the questions, these are people whose faith is deeply woven into the way they live and breathe. They are the 'bread and butter' Christians, the 'salt of the earth' sort, who are thoroughly human, ordinary and safe for it. Their religion hasn't become a weapon to keep the world away or to inflict damage on others. It is an inner rhythm beating alongside their hearts.

BUT HOW CAN YOU TAKE SERVICES OUTSIDE THE CHURCH?

Conventional Christians will have heard a thousand sermons in which the preacher has reminded them that the church is not bricks and mortar but people!

In gardens, homes, on hillsides, boats, beauty spots, across the country groups of people gather. Friends and family come together, many of them strangers to one another, but they come as crowds came to Jesus. Together they choose to take part in an act of worship. They read scripture, say prayers, declare their beliefs. They are the church.

This is the church of the spirit. It knows no walls, no systems of religion; it has no membership cards.

THE TRAPPED AND THE FREE

When Jesus lived, the religion of the day had become so rule-bound, over-organised, political and structured that the Spirit of God had been squeezed out. Corruption flowed through its veins as a disease.

His wide open, relaxed and spontaneous approach to faith shocked the authorities. He was seen as a mad and dangerous man acting disrespectfully both to God and God's chosen representatives.

The people didn't think so, however. Religion came to life again for them. Jesus handed back to the ordinary folk permission to believe and to pray in a way that made sense for them. He taught them about God and how to worship at home, in open spaces and in their hearts.

The power of faith and its usefulness for life became available. It was as though truth had broken free. Inside the religious institution of the Jewish faith, the priests and officials were terrified! Their positions and their power were under threat. For once people had tasted the real thing; there was no going back.

HOME BASED

A lot of people either forget or don't realise that the early 'Christians' and followers of Jesus didn't 'go to church'. They were small clusters of people who gathered together because they wanted to pray and to believe as Jesus had done. They met at each others' homes, on their roof terraces, by the lakes and rivers, in the countryside.

There were no buildings, no formal organisation, no system of priests in charge of everything, no rules. All of that came later. As it came, something vital and necessary began to be lost: the freedom of the Spirit to guide and to move.

SAFETY IN RULES

Some of my critics say that, unlike a parish priest, I am unaccountable — no one is checking up on me.

It should be known that I am not against rules and guidelines. The million dollar question, however, is who sets them. The trouble with the Church is that it exists to protect itself and all its rules are in-house. The parish priests are a law unto themselves. They can almost do what they like except where sex and money come in. Otherwise they can tyrannise their people, conduct themselves inappropriately and rudely and reign over their parishes in a cruel and unchristian manner for years, and no one can do a thing about it.

I, on the other hand, am directly accountable to the public. If I began to do odd, dubious or dangerous things then it would soon become known and my ministry would fail. As with Jesus, so with me, it is the people who decide, not the institution.

True, the authorities conspired to have Jesus killed, but

his spirit lived on, because love can never be destroyed. It lives on and fuels and drives the hearts of those it touches and no amount of devious tactics or strategy can remove it.

NO PRETENSIONS

The fact that I refer back to Jesus does not mean that I am in any way suggesting I am a new Jesus figure! However, his attitude to faith and religion should be emulated by those who follow him.

If you look at the Christian religion today as practised in Britain, it is almost identical to the Judaism of Jesus' day — over-structured and over-regulated. Even the modern churches which stand for a free and spirit-based approach are like prisons in the way they market a precise code of belief and conduct.

So, I want this book to encourage those people of God who want to walk towards the Jesus of the hill top, who want to meet with the early Christians of the front room, who want to carry on the journey that they were taking before it was hijacked down the institutional road.

YOU MARRIED US SO PLEASE COULD YOU BAPTISE OUR BABY?

Relationship brings faith alive. The love that draws us together forges invisible bonds across the years. How many times have I heard about people who have gone back to the church they were married in, or to the priest who married them, because they were hoping for further ministry. How many times have those priests replied, 'But you have moved,' or, 'I have moved,' and therefore you should go to your new church or new priest. Important and beautiful links that have been created are passed over in favour of supporting a system which continually asks people to make new contacts, which of course they rarely do.

One of the beautiful sides of my new approach to ministry is that I am not geographically bound. I will travel anywhere. There are families with whom I've been involved since I began work as a priest in 1982.

I have married them, baptised their babies, buried members of their family, married them a second time and so on. I have a relationship across the decades which gains more meaning and depth with every passing year and event and I provide a figure of security and nourishment for faith through the twists and turns of life.

22 THE CATHEDRAL OF SKY AND MOUNTAIN

A baptism is the most wonderful service to take because its focus is the miracle of life, a unique and precious child given as a gift to the world.

It is extraordinary that most parish priests regard baptisms as a nuisance and the families who come for them as spongers and parasites.

In the past the church taught that every baby had to be baptised. It was almost a part of the process of birth. This habit became so ingrained that even now, decades later, it is an instinctive part of many families' expectations. However, a shock awaits them! Nowadays most vicars have a different view. If you are a club member and attend church often, all well and good; but if you only turn out occasionally or not at all, expect to be sent away with the proverbial flea!

The policy is one of bribery and blackmail. You either need to come to church every week for six months or to go through a 'brainwashing' course involving instruction sessions, videos at home with church members and a final vetting session with the priest to see whether you've swallowed enough to get you hooked. If you have, you're through; if you fall along the course, you're back to square one!

TEARS AND TORMENT

I've had a stream of irate, distraught mothers and fathers on the phone to me having been incensed by their local vicars. Do such vicars actually believe they are doing good service to the gospel or their church by creating such bad feeling in the community?

Anyway, up and down the land, there are countless families who have suffered such treatment. I meet entire families where for two or even three generations children have remained unbaptised because of a rigid priest. The only message that the families take away with them following such encounters is one of rejection and hurt – and this at a time of such hope and promise.

THE CRACKPOT SYSTEM

Mind you, if you do manage to get through the security cordon (which of course some families do, either through conformity or by lying), you are then faced with a fairly unpleasant experience.

The baptism service takes place in the main morning service with about three or four other families. The church is full of newcomers, for most of the regulars can't stand the disruption of the baptism Sunday and stay away. Many of the children aren't used to being in church, bang their heads on the pews, roam noisily and create havoc! The service is often a communion which seems endless and peculiar because it's all about chewing someone's body and sipping blood!

It's an hour and a half of bedlam, with screaming children and a conveyor belt for the baptism. Most of what happens has nothing to do with your reason for being there and is an embarrassment for your guests; you leave the nightmare experience fraught and dissatisfied. The celebration of your unique child and its introduction to faith has been reduced to a cattle market of impersonal rantings.

WHY OH WHY?

Such a system is devised by priests on the defensive. Under threat, their way of packaging and marketing faith is in decline. Numbers are falling, popularity is waning, something has to be done.

In committees they thrash out ideas together. New systems are justified quoting the Bible and theology. Baptisms, weddings and funerals are the times that people in need make contact with the church. Here's the chance to catch them one way or another. If they want something from us, then we'll expose them to an intensive publicity drive. It's like those time-share holiday offers, where you have to go through hours of hard sell tactics before you can get your 'free' gift.

Neighbouring parishes are given the task of policing each others' systems. A refugee from one parish is certainly not given asylum in another! 'You must go to your own priest and do what he says,' the escapee is told.

The unexpected result is a massive meltdown. People dislike the established church even more as they find such tactics patronising and offensive. They are adults with integrity who know what they believe and why. They won't be bullied or manipulated into the beliefs of the local priest acting as a tin pot dictator.

THE BATTLE OF VIEWS

In past years the balance of power has rested with the institutions. State or Church dictated what the options were and everyone had to jump to order. Even when it could be seen to be blatantly unfair, there was nothing that could be done.

The royal family were allowed to have baptisms at home but everyday folk had to go to church. Even if the royals rarely went to church and didn't have a conventional set of beliefs, it didn't matter; they could be baptised, married, anything, as and when and where they wanted.

So in an age of choice, when at its most banal you can buy almost anything from the superstores, why can't you choose the way you want your beliefs expressed? Gone, thankfully, are the days when people were burnt at the stake for their beliefs; gone, too, should be the days when ministry is controlled by the Church.

THE WORLD IS YOUR
OYSTER

So I say to a family, 'It's up to you. You can have your service wherever you would like, at home, in your garden, at work, in a pub, up a mountain, by a lake, in a church, on a boat, the sky's the limit.'

And I say to a family, 'It's up to you. The words of the service must reflect what you believe, what holds value for you and has meaning in your lives. The words must be a reflection of your inner selves and thoughts.'

And I say to a family, 'It's up to you. How do you want me to take the service? How do you want it arranged? What do you want me to wear? In fact, tell me every detail. I'll offer my skills in setting out lots of ideas and choices before you, mingle those with your own and create what is yours.'

The end result is, in the main, a service which is fairly conventional and mainstream Christian in terms of content and style, fine tuned to the couple's approach and refreshing in its mix of new and old material. The venues too are generally not bizarre, ranging from exquisite rooms to private homes to the fine gardens of country estates. Nevertheless, those who want something more extreme can go for it!

The freedom I make available to people to create a service which is right for them is a pioneering form of ministry in this country. Far from compromising the Christian faith, it more truly expresses it.

THE GENUINE ARTICLE

So many services in churches have lost their meaning altogether, because the words no longer arise from the hearts of the worshippers. They are yesterday's words which very often do not carry today's sentiments or wisdom.

What I appreciate about my new ministry is that the people have chosen those words which have meaning for them. I send them suggestions which they can react to, amend, edit, add to or discard altogether. In the to and fro of words a service is born which is 100% the outward expression of an inner understanding. The service I am taking is truth.

OPENING DOORS

This approach creates a sense of relaxation. The families

are not on edge, suspicious and threatened; after all, it's happening at their own home or another venue they've chosen. They are in control and they know their guests aren't going to be embarrassed or bored silly.

Their hearts are wide open to enjoy what happens, to receive the experience of worship and prayer. In the quietness and in the intense moments of the service, such as the signing of the cross on the child's forehead, the baptism itself or the giving of the candle, people are visibly moved.

There is an intimacy and a focus to the event which isn't destroyed by the fidgeting of the restless feet of a bored congregation. I've even seen the tough cookie types who wouldn't be seen dead in a church touched by the experience.

HOLINESS FOR EVERYONE

It used to annoy me intensely when Christian people encouraged the notion that there is something super holy about a church or its sanctuary, as though you could capture holiness in a space.

Holiness is of the spirit and everything has the potential for holiness. It thrills me to transform a front room, a back garden, a hotel room or a pub into a holy place. It emphasises the point that God is not locked up in the parish church.

After the ceremony the family can watch on video their room, their home having been turned into a church, or they can close their eyes and see the cross, the shining font, the beautiful vestments and feel the love that filled them that day.

God visited their house and now God's there to stay.

23 FROM CLOUD TO CIRCUS RING

It had to be the most wonderful setting possible for a baptism. We had climbed from the foot of Mount Snowdon to its peak on a fine and clear day. The views were breathtaking with distant horizons on every side. The colours and contours were vivid and the air was soft and warm.

We found an outcrop of rocks and set up a cross, candlesticks and a font. My vestry was a precarious slope. The guests perched down on grass and stone and we were quiet awhile, soaking up the wonder, bathing in the glory.

No cathedral or church could ever have compared with this majesty. Thus took place the first baptism upon the summit of Mount Snowdon.

It seemed so appropriate to have found a place from which one could look down on the petty rules and squabbles of religion and be free, soaring high in our spirits above those things which restrict and cramp our freedom and our inspiration.

AN ELEPHANT NEVER VISITED MY CHURCH

The most unusual venue for a baptism at ground level was in a circus big top. The director wanted his daughter to be baptised and, following a continental tradition, wanted the service under canvas.

I set up the font on the sawdust of the ring, with the empty circus seats filled with the silent delight of all those who had watched and laughed and loved the shows.

Slowly the circus family began to arrive. The clown made up with broad smile and comic relief nose; the trapeze artists glittering in a thousand sequins, jugglers, acrobats and, last of all, the 26-year-old circus elephant — all came into the ring!

I had never before had such a congregation. As I read the prayers, one word kept coming to me: 'incarnation'. It's a fancy word for describing the belief that God appeared in human form in Jesus. It's about God, not staying hived off in heaven but being found near us and in us and around us.

CULTURAL TYRANNY

I thought to myself how awful it would have been to have forced this group of people to attend their local parish church. They would have been robbed of their cultural setting and the life they cherished and squeezed into the cultural mould of the church.

Instead, here we were celebrating the baptism in their cultural home. God was not locked up in some cold and empty building but was to be found in the circus ring, in the circus family and in their way of life.

RUGBY, DARTS AND BEER

Then there have been the memorable services in the pub.

On one occasion I had been invited to baptise four children at a pub in south east London. I knew the area well. The church was struggling and stood nearby, rarely used and irrelevant to most of the community.

In contrast the pub was the hub of the community, bristling with vitality. It was packed that Saturday afternoon. The bar rooms were crowded; many were watching the rugby while others played pool or darts. Groups of joking friends spilled into the garden while others sat enjoying the sun.

The baptism was to be held in the centre of the lawn and about a hundred chairs were arranged facing a centrepiece of flowers. Well, I knew where Jesus would have been that day, given the choice: the church wouldn't have got a look in.

THE SUPERNATURAL

Many people spend their lives chasing spooks, ghosts and a world 'out there'. The supernatural holds a fascination. What people haven't realised is that magic and mystery lie within the folds of what is natural and ordinary.

Dreams are realised and wishes come true not with magic wands but when people unlock the potential within themselves and within life.

Worship in a pub is like that: taking the ordinary everyday environment and lifting people's eyes to see what's there all the time. As the service progressed, heads hung round the pub door, quizzical eyes peered through glass, something enticed others to gather, watch and listen.

I often think that the regulars will always remember the day God visited the pub. Others will have a sense that he drinks with them every night.

THE TELLTALE CIGAR

The first home baptism I did is etched for ever in my

mind. I can remember the dad handing out beers before the ceremony and passing by with a cigar, filling the room with its rich and heavy smoke.

Something in me ruffled: 'But this is a baptism — he shouldn't be smoking.' I paused and then my worry was removed by a much greater sense of joy which began to fill me. This man, these people, feel at home, relaxed and happy to be themselves. They are not frozen, nervous about whether they are doing the right or wrong thing in the church. God has come to visit them and loves them and accepts them just as they are.

I often chuckle to myself and imagine the faces of churchgoers if a baptism family pulled a four-pack out of their bag to share along the pew!

SPECIAL NEEDS

Then there have been the families with problems of various kinds: a precious child with a terminal illness; an autistic child; one with behavioural problems; a mother with agoraphobia; a complicated family background; parents with sight or hearing difficulties. In these situations the service can be sensitive and thoughtful. The words, for instance, can be adapted; necessary pauses can be made if the baby's hungry or a nappy needs changing; unrestrainable children can roam. Whatever the problems, they can be accommodated.

I've been called out to do emergency baptisms in the night, been baptised myself by mischievous children before I managed to sprinkle them, and had to stop my silver oil pot being hurled as a missile across the room.

THE GARDENS OF GOD

Some of the loveliest services have been outside in people's gardens. I can remember a number where the flowers have been laden with blossom and the service has been beside a pond or water fountain.

In the quietness, the sound of running water accompanied by a medley of birdsong under a balmy sun has been the perfect setting to celebrate and give thanks for a child. The heavy symbols of church have been replaced by something which for the guests feels much closer to God, and they are moved accordingly.

ACROSS THE BOUNDARIES

There is no discrimination in my work. I am available for anyone and everyone. On one day I can visit a country estate where champagne flows like water and the child to be baptised arrives in horse and trap and then move on to a one-bedroomed flat where a single mother struggles to cope. Everyone's circumstances are different, but their hearts and their needs are the same.

We all long for love and acceptance. I intend that to be the essence of my ministry. As a Christian priest, I have been called to offer just that.

THE SERVICE ITSELF

I hope that I take all my services in a personal manner. My aim is to create an easy and comfortable feeling in which people are able to relax. The dynamic of the service needs to work hand in glove with the events of the moment. If people need to move, children make comments or cameras flash, none of it poses a problem.

Everything can be woven into the service and within this practical, hands-on approach; moments of mystery, of wonder, of the sense of God's presence, emerge naturally. The service never rules the occasion; it is a servant to the family and expresses for them the love and hope which is at the heart of the gathering.

CONVENTIONAL OR WACKY?

The interesting thing is that the majority of my ministry is 'conventional'. True, the venues and the approach may be different, but in terms of what actually happens on the day, the content of the service is bread and butter Christian worship.

Even when people want something less 'churchy' they end up having something quite acceptable to the Christian mainstream, though the words may be more colloquial and informal.

A small number of families want something other than a baptism, perhaps a naming or a blessing ceremony, a chance to give thanks for their baby and to dedicate its life to God or towards goodness. Such services are equally meaningful.

HISTORICAL DOCUMENTS

As this is a pioneering form of ministry and the beginning of a new approach in this country, it has been important to keep meticulous registers. Every baptism is entered properly in baptism registers and every service in service registers.

The contents of the baptism registers are unique. Each page entry is devoted to a particular parish across the land and after four years I have five such books. When I die they will be lodged at the County Record Office with other parochial records.

The service registers demonstrate the extent of my ministry, the range of services performed and the numbers of those attending. They make fascinating reading and will, I hope, entertain future researchers!

24 BREAKING THE CHURCH–STATE MONOPOLY

How often have you heard someone in despair saying, 'I don't want a church wedding but the registry office is so awful. If only I could . . .'? It has always seemed madness to me that people are prevented from having their dream wedding. In such situations my instinctive response is always that there must be a way.

When I began my new ministry I provided such a way for people. For the first time there was someone who was willing to offer a full and complete wedding cere-mony in an entirely flexible manner. I can remember one of my first couples saying that they had looked for months for such a person. It was three weeks before their wedding day and they had just read about me. 'It was our dream come true,' they said.

UNLOCKING THE AVIARY

When couples phone or visit me and tell me their hopes and ideas, it's wonderful to be able to say, 'Yes.' Their imaginations are released and they can set about creating a beautiful occasion.

It has been the traditional wisdom to deny such free-dom because of the fear that such licence would lead to all sorts of dangerous innovations threatening society. What rubbish! As artists are protective and proud of their work, a couple's plans arise from deep within them. Their wedding isn't a trivial gimmick but a carefully worked expression of their individuality.

BUT THAT'S JUST CRAZY!

Of course, for some people, your ideas may appear bizarre or awkward because they don't inhabit the world or experience from which you come. I remember a local vicar commenting sourly when he heard about an unusual wedding, 'Well, silly people do silly things.' It is just such prejudice which has choked the life and vitality of people across the generations and has led to the decline in people's interest in church or state.

Censure and disdain are the techniques used by small people to protect their territory. In today's world it only humiliates the critics, for they have lost their power to prevent or spoil another's dream.

THE LAW IS SOMETIMES
AN ASS!

As far as weddings go that's certainly true. Even with recent changes it is still hopelessly restrictive. Most couples when planning their perfect wedding come to a dead end and turn back with disappointment, but I was sure there was a way.

I can advise couples now on a range of different ways they can link the legal and ceremonial parts of their wedding day. At certain venues, if the couple desire, the Registrar can fulfil the legal aspects of the wedding and then once he or she has left, a religious or secular service can follow.

However, the most popular choice is what I call the 'continental approach'. It is the simplest to arrange and gives the couple the maximum freedom. I introduced the idea when I began my new ministry and it instantly caught on. Across the continent they adopt a different, two-tier system for marriage. Couples must first go to register their wedding legally at the municipal building and then afterwards on the same or often another day they have their wedding service with family and friends.

So if the law is acting like an ass then treat it like one! I suggest to couples that they follow the same procedure. In the week before they would go to the Registry Office. There they should have arranged to carry out the barest minimum of ritual. Basically, there are no frills like music or readings, not even the exchanging of rings. They answer the mandatory questions and sign the papers. As witnesses, they take either two close members of the family or friends. Some arrange for myself and my personal assistant, or two others who are unconnected with them, to attend.

THE JEANS JOB

One couple told me of how they dashed in five minutes late, she in a bikini top and he in shorts. They rushed it through and were in and out in six minutes. They imagined the Registrar's thoughts as they left: 'Oh, the young people of today, no respect even for marriage!' What they knew was that the next day they were having the most elaborate and carefully planned wedding ever!

Some people still choose to make this part special in its own way, while reserving the main focus for their service with me, but most couples treat it like slipping into the bank to carry out some paper work. For them it has no significance or importance. Although it is legally their wedding, for them their true wedding is what we have planned together with their families and friends. It is that day which will be celebrated for the coming years as their wedding anniversary.

Of course, having carried out the legal wedding, there are absolutely no restrictions as to what the couple can plan. Their wedding can be in the form, at the venue and in the manner of their choosing.

REGAINING THE INITIATIVE

There is nothing quite so odious to me as having to sit through a service which has no meaning. It is like attending a wedding of convenience, where the couple have no love for each other. Something is happening outwardly but inside it's hollow, an empty shell.

Laws and regulations often coerce people into going through the motions just because there is no other way.

My 'continental approach' allows couples to chuck what's of no use to them on the scrap heap and to create something where a lovely harmony exists between what they feel and what they are doing and saying.

TEARS TO THE EYES

Over the years I have developed a wedding booklet of material for wedding services. It is a unique document and the couples with whom I work read through this together.

It is full of beautiful words and poetry, traditional and modern material, standard and alternative vows, readings, prayers; in fact every resource to create a perfect wedding. Of course they can also adapt, edit, discard or add to the material. It is infinitely flexible. What matters in the end is that the words chosen for their service will convey for them what they believe about love, marriage and God.

A number have said that they couldn't read it without

crying, so lovely were the sentiments, and that sharing it together was an intimate experience for them.

THE NORMAL CONVEYOR BELT

So much thought and care is invested in a wedding, not to mention money! Every detail is pored over exhaustively — except for what happens in the church. Over this the couple have little or no choice. They can't choose the vicar, who may be wonderful but could be ghastly. They can't choose their service or the way it is conducted.

How strange this is when it forms such a vital part of the day! Sometimes the wedding goes well, but many times the reception is a hotbed of analysis as the guests try and shake off the cobwebbed feelings about the dire service they've just attended so that they can enjoy the rest of the day.

THE OBSTACLE COURSE

It's amazing when you consider what they have had to endure to book the church. They may have had to be baptised and confirmed, or attended the church for six months or several weeks; they may have had to attend a preparation course, the worst of which are run by the vicar.

Of course, it is worse still if either or both were divorced. Then they would have faced a humiliating interview and rejection or a prolonged form-filling exercise and an interminable wait while the bishop and his cronies pass judgment on whether the marriage could go ahead.

In some cases, it may be all plain sailing but what still remains a worrying unknown is what the church bit will be like on the day.

WHAT WOULD YOU LIKE
ME TO WEAR?

It always surprises couples when I ask them what I should wear. Every detail is their choice. Do they want me to bring a cross, or the candlesticks? Do they want me robed? If so, do they want just the cassock and surplice, or the full works?

Do they want other people involved in the service or just me? Do they want to sing – hymns or anything else? I take them through the entire ceremony and they sculpt out of the raw material their desired event.

OTHER FAITHS, NO FAITH

Some couples come where one partner is Christian and the other is of another religion.

It is an expression of love to be able to provide for them a service which incorporates both traditions. They either want someone else to lead the sections from another faith, or ask if I would be willing to do it. It causes me no problem. Love is willing to respect and handle sensitively and reverently the treasures of another person. How could it be otherwise? How could God want me to do otherwise? At one wedding I was proud to wear my cassock with a Jewish *yarmulke*.

Likewise if a person wants a service without the clutter of religious words and imagery, then why should that be difficult? I have never had a person who didn't want a service which celebrated and honoured love and care and commitment. If what is good in life is available for use in such a service then as far as I am concerned as a priest, God is very fully involved. I don't need to keep bleating God's name, or the contents of the religious linguistic cupboard.

25 THE INTERNET, SPEEDBOATS, APPLE ORCHARDS AND CASTLES

The wind was strong but the sky was blue as we roared out onto the English Channel. The jetty off Littlehampton harbour was busy with wedding guests peering out at us across the water. Even the Registrar, who had been bemused the day before to learn that their 'real' wedding was happening the next day on a speedboat, had turned out to watch.

The bride and groom were in full attire, I wore my elaborate gown, and with a handful of guests we were clinging discreetly on to the sides of the speedboat which, although it had come to rest, still persisted in lurching from side to side.

That was my first taste of something quite 'unusual'.

THE FIRST UK WEDDING OVER THE INTERNET

This was a laugh! The happy couple were named Dawn Raid and Dragan Radosevolich. They had met over the Internet, had courted via e-mail and had finally touched flesh in a London pub. Altogether they liked what they saw and went ahead with plans for a cybernet wedding.

I was in one Cybercafé bar in Ealing and they in another in central London. The visuals were done over the net and the sound courtesy of British Telecom. The computer nuts loved it, as did Dawn and Dragan. Some might have feared it would be impersonal, but it was not. The service they chose was deep and beautiful and they, with others, were moved to tears and to laughter through the service.

THE WETTEST WEDDING

The couple had met under a boat in Cyprus! What then could have been better than holding the wedding underwater?

It certainly felt strange wearing my beautiful robe as I led the bride along the water's edge. Stranger still was when, half way through the service, I swapped the robe for the necessary scuba gear.

Fully oxygenated and dog-collared I led the couple and their attendants down beneath the water, to the altar and candles below. We were using the latest sound equipment which enabled us to hear each other and so they made their vows to one another.

The only tricky moment came when the groom, overcome with emotion, snatched the bride's breathing apparatus away to kiss her, and almost drowned her in the process!

THE APPLE ORCHARD

It was like something from a Hardy novel: young girls skipped along the country lane through rye grass and poppy flowers, and a straggling band of wedding pilgrims made their way to an apple orchard tucked away in the heart of the Kent countryside.

It was a wonderful day: a broad blue sky with wisps of

cloud, butterflies chasing the scents and startled hares bounding across the fields. Here amidst nature's glory we celebrated the wedding.

THE CASTLE RUINS

Grannies and aunts and uncles gathered alongside leathered and tattooed youngsters whose machines had raged together in the car park — an unlikely group for a Saturday afternoon inside the walls of Newark Castle.

After a long wait another roar could be heard and Duke pulled into the castle grounds on his low-slung dragster bearing the bride, dressed as Morticia from the Addams family.

It was uncanny. The service, the setting, the scene was perfect — grand, alternative and yet simple. It cost hardly anything and yet probably surpassed the most elaborate weddings. The couple were certainly alternative, but they had so much wanted a priest to be there to share with them the meaningful words they had chosen.

I chuckled to myself. As I swept up to the great stone windows overlooking the Newark valley in my embroidered gown, leading 'Morticia' to her husband-to-be , I thought how much I preferred being there rather than stuck in some cathedral or church where those inside would only turn their noses up at such a couple.

THE FREEDOM TO BE

I always calm couples by assuring them that they have nothing to worry about through the service; that I will guide them from start to finish. Having said that, I also stress that my guiding the proceedings is not a straitjacket; they should feel entirely free to do or say whatever they want. Nothing, I bravely say, would ever throw me, because I'd weave anything that happened into the service.

Most couples are happy to be guided, but some will

make joking remarks to one another or to their guests. I had one bride who, having kept her guests waiting 20 minutes, stepped out of the wedding car onto the lawns of the country hotel and with a wave of her hand declared, 'Hya, folks!' When I asked whether she wanted to take her intended as her husband, she paused cheekily, stepped back, gave him the once over and then somewhat questioningly replied, 'Yeeees'!

After all, this is their big day and their service. I love them to make of it what they choose.

FROM MILKING SHEDS TO COUNTRY BARNS

Some people find the most wonderful settings for their services.

One wedding was held in a converted milking shed, lined with the original beams and whitewashed, burgeoning with flowers. A quartet provided the music and the bride arrived over the cobbled forecourt.

Another was held in an ancient Norman chapel, lit by candles and laden with daffodils, while peacocks strutted proudly on the lawns outside.

Another took place in what used to be a vast chapel but was now converted into a banqueting suite, with the original sanctuary still preserved. The colours from the stained glass windows enveloped the guests in a rainbow light.

Another was on the shores of Lake Windermere, with forested backdrop and swans gliding by to order!

Castle rooms, country barns, river cruisers, hillsides, back gardens, hotel suites, football stadiums, anywhere and everywhere, weddings have been celebrated.

A LONDON PARK

Midsummer, under a dusky sky, within a circle of flaming

torches and watched by a group of wide-eyed children was a very individual setting for one wedding. The couple really wanted it to be very informal and even largely unscripted!

The service was to pass through four stages, interspersed with popular songs, but while each stage had a heading I had to speak spontaneously. It was the only service I have taken for which I travelled with no text!

In addition they wanted me to wear my dog collar and a Hawaiian shirt which, as my wardrobe couldn't oblige, they provided.

A SELECTION OF FOREIGN JAUNTS

Some people want to pack a priest in their suitcase as well! Weddings in exotic, romantic or significant settings with an English priest is for some the perfect mix. I've travelled out to Loutro in Crete to take a wedding in a beautiful village Orthodox church, although the bride wasn't quite expecting the elderly ladies of the village to swarm round her during the service tugging at her dress and gossiping loudly as was their tradition!

I've taken a lovely wedding out in Minorca, where the groom's spanking new silk tie was unexpectedly cut off and up and sold by auction, as is their tradition!

Marrakesh, under the Atlas mountains, was an awesome and spectacular setting for a service. It was certainly unusual, with a band of snake charmers, acrobats and dancers ready to perform as soon as the ceremony finished.

TOUCHING VENUES

Some have wanted to return to childhood haunts. One such wedding was held underneath a willow tree on an island surrounded by canal waterways. It was here that the bride had played as a child while her mother worked at the adjoining mill.

Family homes and gardens, the night club or a venue where romance blossomed or where special holidays had been taken are favourite choices.

SURPRISE, SURPRISE!

Some manage to build in the element of surprise even to the wedding itself. One bride arranged, unbeknown to her partner, for the actual wedding and reception to be held at his beloved Chelsea football ground. Another considered holding a service at half time during the women's rugby match in which she would have been playing.

Some have planned a service during a function at which the invited guests had no idea what would happen.

MAKING THE ORDINARY EXTRAORDINARY

Most of the services I take are quite conventional, however. Of course the setting and the content of the service is chosen by the couple and bears their unique mark, but their wish is for the wedding to be experienced by their guests as a traditional wedding with walk down the aisle, vows, rings and signing the register.

This is bread and butter priestly work, but releasing it from the killing restrictions of tradition and church rules and approaching it with flexibility and the refreshment of the couple's close involvement gives the whole experience a marvellous lift. The wedding is transformed into something living and real. Gone are the cobwebs of a bygone system; instead we adopt an approach which makes sense and fills the occasion with meaning and significance.

Of course, for some, their desire is to make the setting tingle with individuality as well. The hotel, garden, banqueting suite is too limiting. For them it has to be a cruise liner, Concorde or floating in the blue and open sky in a hot air balloon!

26   LOVE AGAINST ALL ODDS

You sometimes read about a priest who has been willing to carry out a 'hole in the corner' blessing for a gay or lesbian couple. They are terrified of what their congregations or colleagues might say if they are found out. Other priests refuse point blank.

It's tragic when you reduce people's deep and rich experience into something they have to hide or something about which they are mistakenly made to feel ashamed.

When a gay or lesbian couple contact me they are assured of exactly the same care and respect as I would give to a heterosexual couple. Love wherever it is found is to be valued and protected.

YOU CAN'T . . .

Many people enjoy being able to say, 'You can't!' They feel powerful and more secure by being able to declare what can and can't be done. They feel that their world would fall apart if they said, 'Yes, you can!' All sorts of terrible things might happen!

Not so. The world becomes a safer place when each

allows others to journey towards their light, especially when that light is love.

Some of the most moving and meaningful services I have done have been for gay or lesbian couples, who have had to struggle to survive, who have faced untold pressures and hostility, and who have learnt the pain of owning their individuality in a conformist world.

THE TRUE COMMUNITY

There is something special when mums and dads, grandparents, aunts and uncles gather with friends and colleagues from many walks of life for the wedding of two women or two men. They have grown accustomed to and recognised the undeniable beauty of a relationship which they want to see blossoming into the commitment of marriage.

I heard about a preacher recently who although sympathetic to such couples warned that they shouldn't 'imitate or mimic' heterosexual marriages. That is to miss the point. It is not imitation, it is the natural end of intimate love forged between two people.

One lesbian couple told me that whereas they had resisted the idea of marriage for ten years, their parents had kept pressing them towards it.

THE TUTTING CHURCH

Just before one lesbian wedding I did, I had heard a Christian woman broadcasting an 'anti gay' *Thought for the Day* on Radio 4. In contrast to her life-denying and defensive opinions, the wedding service was full of warmth and love. There were no dry eyes as the couple clasped one another and, with a resolve already tested through time and trouble, they pledged their eternal love for each other.

The pathways of their lives had brought them to this

moment. Treasures each had collected along the way were entrusted to the other. Their individuality and unique journey were affirmed and celebrated by the guests. This was a loving, nourishing and nurturing community at its best.

The church that morning had remained cloistered in the shadows of prejudice, broadcasting dark sentiments to shackle and chain its listeners. Here we were free, blossoming in the liberty of love and acceptance.

As I took the service I could hear in my thoughts the Mothers' Union, readers and priests, the regular church-goers (often the very worst sort) tut tutting to themselves as they preened their feathers of self-righteousness.

SECRETIVE AND SAUCY CHURCHWARDENS

Never imagine things are as they seem! You scan a morning congregation and see a mass of fine upright 'cleaner than clean' citizens. If you haven't used a spiritual form of washing powder then it's certainly an incentive to start. Let's all play at being whiter than white.

It's a lie, of course.

I remember when a churchwarden, from another church, came to me. He lived with his wife and his children working faithfully in the church and holding a 'respected' and secure place in the church's life.

During his visit he told me of his homosexuality, of his regular visits to gay bars and his one-off sexual encounters with those he picked up. It was a complex and involved world within which he lived. No one else in the church knew anything about it. Such is the nature of expectation. It shoves those who fall from its fickle grasp underground, into the dark tunnels and passages of life in which they seek an acceptance they can never find.

The churchwarden wanted me to absolve him, accept and affirm him, hold him and hug him and send him away back into his lonely world of deceit and lies.

Next time you look round a congregation, weep for the broken and the lost and the fractured lives that can never know healing or peace, whose white shirts and frocks hide the wounds which bleed or fester unrecognised and untended.

IT'S ABOUT TIME

One can wait a lifetime for attitudes to change and for things to become possible. One can reach the grave disappointed and angry with others for having denied you your dream. Never let that happen to you.

Any dream which has value can come true.

So don't sit around and wait for others to give permission; say 'yes' to and for yourself. Such has been the attitude of many of the gay and lesbian couples I have known and whom I have encouraged. Pieces of paper from the state, legal recognition, acceptance in the community, approval from the church — these are some of the games which the power brokers make us play. By joining in, you only enhance their authority.

If the rules of others are crude enough not to accommodate you, chuck them. Play the game of life with better rules that involve and include everyone. Imbue them with the authority vested in yourself as a unique and precious member of the community. See them worked, modified, accepted and respected by others around you.

If a gay or lesbian couple want a wedding ceremony and want to regard themselves as a married couple, then that is for them to believe and them to know. Those who love and respect them will affirm them. My role as a priest is to assist them and to serve them in naming their reality and in fulfilling their dream.

ALWAYS BIN
A GENERALISATION

All my working days I have worked with people at the cutting edge of their lives, at the place where pretence gives way to truth. In my time every prejudice and assumption has been challenged and so many stereotypes have been broken.

There are as many kinds of people as people themselves and as many kinds of relationships as relationships themselves. Our attempt to put everything into neat boxes shows up our fear of life in all its variety. It's satisfying to throw away the boxes and to take each situation anew. We then keep the wide-open eyes of childhood, able to see and appreciate, uncorrupted by cynicism and boredom.

It allows us to peel off the layers of conformity that have often suffocated us and set free our own special self, wonderfully our own and as no other.

SEX AS A
WINDOW TO GOD

Our dreams and our desires are a jungle through which we pass with wonder and caution. It's good not to travel alone, although it's highly dangerous to invite another to travel with you.

In the jungle we discover ourselves, we encounter the other and we become aware of God. It is a precious moment when people begin to tell you about their jungle. They allow you to view their innermost selves, their path from childhood to adulthood and all that has happened along the way. Such is holy ground.

When the church bandies around crude and heavy handed judgments about these areas and issues, it should realise that it silences many people, shuttering their windows and closing their doors. It prevents true 'communion' from ever taking place and turns the church into a superficial gossip hut.

As far as I am concerned, come forward all and sundry, be you straight, gay, lesbian, transvestite, transsexual; whether you are into leather, feathers or Mars bars. Whatever your orientation or your taste, whether it's within the narrow or at the most extreme boundaries known to society, you are welcome and loved unconditionally, as you are.

OVER THE EDGE

Even if you've fallen over the edge into the world of taboo and prohibition, into the dark realms of criminality and abuse, you are still welcome to be loved unconditionally. Not that your actions could meet with my agreement or condoning, but give me your honesty and I will give you my time and my love so that such love could be the light to guide you through your darkness and into a place of safety and benefit for you and for others.

It is my firm belief that no one acts in such a way unless they are genetically so inclined, or unless they have been wounded along the way. In both situations wise, responsible and generous love is required.

WITHIN THE WIDEST BOUNDARIES

This chapter is devoted most specifically to those whose lives and love bring happiness and joy to others, while yet being expressed in alternative or unconventional relationships. All the while the church refuses to minister to such people, it betrays the gospel of love, and misses out on the deep well of experience that such people are only too happy to share.

27 THE COFFIN TRADE

There is a scandalous and damaging trade in death carried on in this country between the undertaking profession and the Church of England.

Put simply, the Church of England has the monopoly on funeral services. The system runs like this: someone dies, their family attend the local undertakers and as most families have no alternative suggestion, the funeral is passed automatically to the local C of E priest.

The Church is eager to protect this system because of course it receives considerable revenue from it. However, because it is a monopoly with no real accountability the general standard of service given is appalling.

If you have been to a funeral service recently you may well be nodding. The priest has had little or no contact with the family and has found out little or nothing about the deceased.

The priest relies heavily upon the service text which, as he delivers it *ad nauseam* week in and week out, becomes a drone of meaningless religio-twaddle for the hearers. For the priest it is yet another service within an already busy week which he or she could well do without.

ALTERNATIVES

Because the system is so well wrapped up by the church it is hard for families to know of any alternatives. Indeed the undertakers themselves find it a tricky situation. I've witnessed many discussions at priests' meetings where plans were being drawn up to contact undertakers with all guns blazing because they were passing funerals to other people who were thus getting the income.

They can often only help if the families themselves request a different priest or person to take the service.

When I began to offer a funeral ministry as an independent priest it exposed the depths to which the church was willing to stoop to act politically to try and safeguard its trade in death. Church officials circulated letters and made phone calls.

Thankfully there are those undertakers who are more concerned for their clients than the system. They were willing to recommend me, and now many families ask for my ministry anyway.

HORROR STORIES

Sometimes I can't believe my ears when families tell of their experiences at the hands of priests – those who turn up late for services, who use the wrong name, who never refer to the deceased, and never even use their name.

Worse, though, are those who want to justify to themselves why they are taking this service anyway. After all, none of the family come to the church, so they turn the funeral into some sort of evangelistic circus – not quite a Billy Graham Crusade but not far off, with heavy doctrine preached and a call given for commitment.

I know of one family who had been devastated when the priest was adamant that their loved one would not be going to heaven because she had never given her heart to

Jesus, and the family must treat the funeral as a chance for them to convert to avoid the same fate.

THE ESSENTIALS IN
TRAGEDY

The family of someone who has died desperately want and need to talk about their loved one. They want to fill the cruel absence that death has forced upon them with the memories, stories and recollection of their loved one.

It is of the utmost importance to me to spend quality time in listening sensitively to the family telling me their stories and, by asking them appropriate questions, to begin to gain a picture and understanding of the life of the deceased.

In fact, this preparation can itself help in the pain of bereavement because it reawakens a host of memories and brings the person's life even more vividly into focus.

THE FUNERAL

I have had many families say to me that whereas they had been dreading the service beforehand they had in fact found it to be a helpful, even healing experience.

What is essential in considering the service is that the text, the prayers and the readings must meet and love the mourners in their need. The text has no importance of its own, other than to serve those attending. The many priests who remain slaves to the text have missed the point.

In funeral services I talk extensively about the bereaved, making them present, bringing them back to life through word and story, sensitively sculpted together. I help make the idea of resurrection real by signalling to the family how they can move from feeling close to the body of their loved one to feeling close to their spirit instead, in the same way that lovers feel close even when separated by many miles. Their loved ones remain present today and tomorrow as they were yesterday, only in a different way.

That form needs to be revealed by the priest in the service and shown to the family so they leave with a sense not only of cruel loss but of a mysterious beckoning, a sense of promise, of a togetherness with their loved one that they must learn about and which holds a greater closeness than even that which they had known.

AND JUST A SPRINKLING OF RELIGIO-SPEAK

Around this carefully presented portrayal of the loved one, the prayers and readings must be placed to cushion and embrace the mourners in their pain. They must be resources as important and as sweet as arms of comfort, a mug of coffee or a good night's sleep. They must be palatable, nourishing and easily digestible. They must make sense.

AN ART FORM

Every service is a work of art, but perhaps none more so than a funeral. Those attending are highly vulnerable and every part of the service needs the most careful attention. It is therefore outrageous that this most acute point of the church's ministry to the public should be carried out in such a routine and insensitive manner.

YOU CAN'T DO THAT!

The priest's tyranny even intrudes into the place of death. We read in the papers about the crass decisions to ban families from using certain names or descriptions from tombstones. So in the services families are told they can't include a particular song, piece of music, reading, flag or organisation.

The priest vets the proceedings, taking care of his/her own feelings and beliefs and putting the family second. Why? The priest is there to serve the people, not to rule over them and coerce them into his/her value judgments and prejudices. If his/her concern is for truth, there can be no greater truth than the requests of the family and the ingredients of the deceased's life.

SKIN DEEP REACTIONS

Surely a priest should be someone who does not go by outward appearance alone and is not quick to jump to conclusions.

I have had a number of families who have come and asked for an atheist service. 'What!' my colleagues have said. 'No mention of God? Impossible!'

But why? From thought or experience, people may have come to reject certain aspects of life either positively or because they have become associated rightly or wrongly with something that has hurt them.

What is of importance is what lies within the heart of those involved. A service which is full of love and lovingly taken need have no religious words whatsoever. I love that Bible passage which says that 'God is love and those who live in love live in God and God lives in them.'

I haven't yet encountered a person who had no use for love, who didn't respond when loved, who wasn't damaged through being denied love. Love is the basic nutrient for our lives, our sunshine and our hope.

If a priest's capacity to love is exhausted when certain words are absent, it is a sorry state of affairs.

28 FROM PETS TO PASSION

When you look at the service books and the types of service offered by the denominational churches, it's hard to believe how unimaginative and limiting is the system of worship on offer.

People today have many varied needs for worship, which arise out of their experience. The frightened priest runs to his or her Prayer Book and finds that there just isn't a service to fit the need — or if there is, it is stiff and out of touch.

There is a vast range of needs. A woman has miscarried and wants a service for her lost child; an elderly couple want to bury their fifteen-year-old family pet; a couple want to renew their wedding vows after ten years; parents want a blessing and dedication service with godparents for their newborn; a group of friends want to share communion in the countryside, an eighteen-year-old wants to mark a special birthday; a graduate wants to celebrate a degree; a family are looking to have their new home blessed. The list of possibilities is endless.

The need for prayer flows naturally from the events of life. The church should provide a ministry designed to weave a spiritual awareness into the fabric of everyday existence. Instead, the services are repetitive and point-less, for they have so little relevance to or connection with people's lives and concerns.

THE DREADED COMMITTEE

The system that all worship material has to be approved by committee and synod indicates the extent of control which officials like to exert over the churches.

What I find exhilarating is to receive a request from a person or family for a particular type of service and then to rise to the challenge of writing and producing something suitable. The process is interactive. The text is viewed by the family whose comments inform the subsequent drafts until I'm left with a service which is alive with the hearts and minds of those for whom it has significance.

The words for worship have been rescued from the fog of church debate and stilted compromise and have been placed back into the mouths of the worshippers. They can speak their own language and not one thrust upon them.

TIMID AND TRAPPED

So often, religious people become boxed in and look nerv-ously over their shoulders lest they have contaminated themselves or their spiritual life with 'unclean' sources.

It's a sad approach to life, which runs counter to a belief in the creativity and diversity of God's activity. Everything is available to include in worship. Art, music, writing, all the different strands of human endeavour and achievement are potential resources.

In tight Christian circles you'll hear the comments, 'But it's not of God, it's not Christian, it can't be used.' Do these people really believe that God is so small as to be trapped inside their world view?

God is to be found in everything. It makes no difference whether something comes from another religious
tradition or from an atheist. What matters is whether it
carries with it the spark of life and light which feeds the
worshipper. If so it can be used gladly.

BUT MINISTRY TO PETS,
THAT'S GOING TOO FAR!

You only have to talk with people who are or have been
devoted to their pets to respect their reverence and love
of their animals. Sometimes we mock such attachments
and the investment of attention that goes into them, but
as with most commitments someone standing watching
from the sidelines is rarely able to understand the mystery
of such a person's experience.

You have to enter the hearts of people to feel and to
understand. You have to see the world with their eyes. In
doing so you appreciate the immense significance of the
pet within the person's or the family's life and history.

When illness strikes or when death finally comes,
prayer, anointing and proper ministry express love both
for the pet and its carers. Such ministry values and
cherishes all that has been known and given in the
relationship that has often spanned many years.

COMMUNION

Some of the most beautiful communion services I have
taken since practising as an independent priest have been
outside in places of natural beauty. The nature of the service has been informal, with those attending being able to
express themselves freely. The services have had a simple
structure, with prayers for everyone to join in as well as
just for the priest. However, some people have walked
around, some remained silent, some have asked questions.
There have been pauses, songs, laughter and quietness.

The sharing of bread and wine has been natural, like passing round a plate of biscuits, but also supernatural in that the experience has been charged with a sense of the closeness of the group and their willingness to accept each other with all their differences, as well as the awareness of that love which is beyond us.

COUNSELLING

Counsellors often do so much damage, particularly when they have little self-awareness and are working from a strong philosophical base.

I enjoy the opportunity of being able to encounter people as they are, with the desire to love them, understand them and walk with them as they understand themselves. So often, people enter counselling with a desire to become different, or for something to happen or to change.

What is the greatest help is to experience being loved and accepted just as you are and thus to come out from the corner and see and own yourself as you are. The quest for 'change' is often a flight from reality; with self-awareness comes a natural growth which takes its own course.

THE DEMON FACTOR

I'm always fascinated when I'm asked to exorcise a house, place or person. People often come with very clear language about what is going on and what they want me to do.

Behind language lie a thousand secrets waiting to be uncovered and a thousand truths waiting to be told. So my first task has always been to try and analyse the situation. When people use the language of religion it is often clear that they can't handle what's happening in their everyday lives.

Priests who go in and clumsily brandish religious symbols around the place like holy water are treading on dangerous ground and can often do more damage than they realise. Only after careful talking and sometimes counselling should the suitcase of religious tricks be opened and a symbolic drama between good and evil ensue.

My most vivid case to date, however, involved exorcising a house on the Yorkshire moors while the wind roared and doors slammed, just like the films!

AND SO MUCH MORE

As a priest I have become involved in so many situations that it is hard to write about them all. Visiting the sick and lonely is a quiet part of my work and at times the most harrowing part is to help and support people, particularly children, preparing to die and at the last to watch with them to the end.

The poor come for assistance, people in financial difficulties come for guidance, I end up acting as accountant, solicitor and advocate for folk in distress. As a priest I must turn any skill or resource I have to help others and that leads me down many different walks of life.

BUT WOULD YOU DO
ANYTHING?

Journalists and others often ask if there are any limits to what I would do. So far I have never been asked to provide a service which didn't make good sense within the lives of the people concerned. In addition, with hardly an exception, I have felt satisfied at the end of the ministry that those involved had achieved and received a wholesome inspiration.

Sometimes things have been somewhat hairy and unforeseen practical problems have arisen. Jeremy

Beadle would love to get his hands on some of the videos. On one occasion the family puppy had managed to gnaw through its tether and came haring out of the house sending candlesticks and cross flying while it jumped up wildly all over the bride's dress, but such scenarios thankfully have been few and far between!

29 MONEY, BUSINESS, CULTS AND OTHER QUESTIONS

When I first began, some sections of the press criticised me for my brochure and suspected that it was making a business out of religion.

Nothing could have been further from the truth. I enjoy trying to do things with efficiency and a professionalism that respects the people who turn to me for ministry. It honours my priesthood and it is an expression of my beliefs.

Good systems which help rather than hinder people are an asset. What so often happens, though, is that the system becomes all important and the people and ideals within it are lost.

I was determined that whatever system I had in place would be continually flexible and responsive to the different needs which people presented. I was pioneering a new form of ministry in the country, and so everything had to be set in place as my work developed.

Initially various agents contacted me wanting me to enter into contracts with them, setting it up very much as a business. That held no interest for me whatsoever. My motivation and my enthusiasm arose from my priesthood and my belief that I was discovering a way to minister in this country with the freedom and freshness essential to the Christian gospel.

THE COSY PACKAGE

The Church of England has been cunning in the development of its employment package. A priest has what is called the freehold and is basically unsackable, has a job for life, is provided with an above average house, has numerous perks including interest-free loans, tax-free heating, lighting and cleaning costs, a non-contributory pension, private health care, sickness benefits, an ample salary and access to additional grant making bodies.

It adds up to a considerable income.

The concept of becoming self-employed and having to provide everything myself was a daunting prospect. It was necessary to be realistic about supporting myself and asking people for appropriate contributions towards my ministry.

Thankfully the first trickle of interest in my work has grown to an enthusiastic response.

INFORMATION AND CHOICE

Over the years I have developed a series of letters which give full information about my ministry and the various services I offer. If people want to book a specific date I can send them a quotation letter which gives the costs involved.

Generally these are accepted by people and they can choose a lower or higher cost depending on how much involvement they want with me prior to the service. However, what is important about my work is having the flexibility to respond to people's differing situations. If anyone has a difficulty with the money then I work out with them what they think can be managed. At times that means I do services for nothing or for a reduced amount. I would never want a family not to be able to have a service because of money, and I try to be sensitive in making sure this doesn't happen.

Income I receive from my ministry supports me in the routine pastoral work, because if someone is sick or in hospital then it's not appropriate or possible to ask for a contribution for my work.

BUT WHO IS YOUR BOSS?

When other priests complain that I am not accountable to anyone, I disagree. I believe I am more accountable than they are. There are parishes across the land where incompetent priests are disliked by their congregations and nothing can be done to remove them.

The truth is there is no effective supervision provided for clergy in the Church of England. In contrast I am directly accountable to the people for whom I provide ministry. If I provide an unprofessional or questionable service, word would soon come out; and as my form of ministry is unique in this country, the media would soon latch onto it.

Personally, I am accountable spiritually as any priest is, to God and to the high Christian standard of unconditional love. If I lost sight of that, the energy and integrity with which I approach my work would quickly drain and I would not be able to provide the spiritual light which gives my ministry its authenticity.

ARE YOU STARTING A CULT?

I am absolutely not starting a cult. There are far too many groups in conflict with one another as it is.

The ministry I offer is far healthier than many parish ministries. It is not possible for people to set up dependent relationships with a 'mobile vicar'. I am available when I am needed but unlike the local vicar I'm not constantly around to be pecked at.

My ministry allows spiritual care to be set in the context of people's everyday lives within their normal circle of friends and colleagues. Their community is a natural one rather than the contrived one of the local church.

BUT YOU ARE NOT ENCOURAGING PEOPLE TO GO TO CHURCH!

Whenever people gather who share Christian belief, they are the church. It's not a matter of 'going to' church but *being* the church and gathering as church. The church is made up of people and is not to be mistaken for the small cluster of people who choose to go to a building on a Sunday morning and call themselves the church.

My ministry helps, encourages and enables people to gather as church far more than they would otherwise have done. After such experiences it may well be that they become more involved in a local gathering of Christians, or it may be that they grow spiritually as individuals, as a family or as a circle of friends.

The obsession the Church of England has with packing its buildings on Sunday mornings has little to do with theology or belief and much more to do with the politics of power, control and money.

Significantly, nearly all of the families with whom I work regard themselves as part of the Christian family.

The mistake being made by many of the denominational churches today is to regard them differently, as 'non-believers', just because they don't fit into their church systems.

PROVIDING WHAT'S TRUE

'But you're in danger of just providing people with what they want, and not what's true!'

If ever such a criticism was appropriate it would be levelled at parish priests and bishops. For years there has been a great cover up about advances in theology and Christian thinking. When the former Bishop of Durham, David Jenkins, spoke about what is ordinary Christian understanding in academic circles, there was outcry among the churches. He was seen as a heretic and blasphemer. The truth is that many bishops and priests have sympathy with his views but wouldn't dare admit it out of fear for their popularity.

Most vicars speak the language their congregations want to hear. Christians look around the supermarket of religion in their neighbourhood and pick out the goods that are right for them. Perhaps it's the smells and bells church, or the raving charismatics, or the hot Protestant preachers. When they go they expect to hear words with which they will agree.

When I offer complete choice to those with whom I work, I only offer that greater respect that is willing to work with anyone of any persuasion and any viewpoint because the differences they exhibit are all a part of God's creativity. As a priest I am called not to show partiality but to love all and everything.

30   LOVED AND CHERISHED

Love is the sunshine of our lives. When we feel loved we grow and blossom as people and as ourselves. Most of our lives are spent tramping the earth to find love; in that search, we meet many who love us — our mothers and fathers, the wider family and friends, our partners or spouses. Within all these relationships we learn about love as a vital ingredient for our well-being.

At some point in the unfolding experiences of love we wake up to the stunning and revealing mystery that the point of our maturing and contentment comes when we are able to love ourselves.

All the love received has been a series of pointers on the journey, signals and prompts. All are designed to guide us to the holy door through which alone we can pass into the place of self-worth and self-love.

THE GARDEN OF JOY

Once we are through the door, the world becomes a safer and altogether happier place. Not only are you suffused with a sense of love and being loved from a source which is reliable — yourself — but also your desire to love is increased.

You become sensitised to love as the honey bee is to pollen. Love is in the air, all around, and you can drink eagerly from family and friends in a new and living way, just as you can pour love over them and over others in generous proportions.

BUT WHAT IS THE WAY TO THIS GARDEN, THIS HOLY DOOR?

There are numerous dead ends, wrong turnings and obstacles designed to keep you from finding your way. Perversely, religion is one such obstacle. It can play havoc with people's lives and leave them guilt-ridden, bowed and despairing.

How dare that be allowed to happen!

As we grow, we are faced with so many competing claims for our attention. Many of them arise from people with vested interests or broken desires. When we succumb to these people innocently, we little realise that we are choosing to be imprisoned by other people's weakness.

The path to maturity is a perilous one, but it is one on which we can stand tall and free, having shaken off many encumbrances and being able to own ourselves as unique individuals as well as being able to know those parts within us which are damaged, weak or wounded.

Progress is made when we can begin to accept who we are, not who we might become or who we would like to be, but who we are. There is nothing more important than owning the reality of what is. I am what I am and who I am.

THE POWER BROKERS

Around you there will be individuals, groups or ideologies which say, 'Well, you are O.K. but if this and if that, you would be better.'

Stuff them! You are what you are.

Love that 'you'. It is the only you there will ever be, or that you will ever have.

BUTTERFLY WINGS

This isn't an argument for apathy or for shutting out the world and blocking everyone else's criticism of you. We can never live as an island and our health is dependent on how we manage to integrate our lives within the community around us.

It is from the position of loving yourself that you can truly listen to and sift the clamour of comments around you and make choices for your life and future. Instead of being crushed by the weight of other people's needs and expectations, you can witness a natural personal metamorphosis and love the newly found freedom which your butterfly wings provide.

CATERPILLAR DAYS

The church prefers maggots and caterpillars. They have less scope for movement and are more easily contained. Being ravenously hungry, they stay close to the food provider.

Control is exercised with a range of do's and don'ts and threatened sanctions — in this world and, more sinister still, in the next. It's a cleverly worked system which feeds off a person's need for love and acceptance.

FLY COLOURFUL AND FREE

As someone who has grown to love yourself and so become able to love others, the world is before you. The colours and contours of all things are visible and the choice is firmly in your grasp as to where you land, what you feed on and whom you will bless.

Plants in the Christian garden may be succulent, but there are so many other gardens, so many wild hedgerows, so much in the world to attract and to nourish, as well as so much to do.

Through wisdom and experience you can measure the stature and learn the content of all things; you can value the good and discard the bad. You are responsible for the precious person that is you, and everything which you consume in every way will affect your growing and your doing.

VITAL INGREDIENTS

Happiness requires generous helpings of common sense. Your body must be treasured with good food, regular exercise, proper sleep and general care. Your mind must be respected too, with stimulating reading, culture, hobbies and good quality discussion.

Your soul and spirit need beauty, silence, reflection, with moments of wonder, awe and hope. Your heart needs good and wholesome relationships, people who respect and love you for yourself, people with whom you can laugh and cry and unlock the potential of the future.

You need to be true to yourself and what is. Never fear reality: it is what is. Fantasy and imagination can play untold tricks and visit you with terror. In the soil of knowing what you are and what is, there grow unimagined possibilities. It is the place where dreams come true.

BEAUTIFUL, GLORIOUS, WONDERFUL YOU

Yes, with your strengths and weaknesses, your successes and failures, your darkness and your light, you have the right to be. You have the right to believe in yourself, to love yourself and to be proud of yourself.

Don't let the soul-killers, the life-haters, the rabid

religio-nuts, the cramping ideologues, the destroying dogmatists, the don't-ers and can't-ers and shouldn't-ers, the 'God says this and the Bible says that'-ers, the 'What would people think'-ers, the control freaks found under every stone and round every corner in every profession and in all walks of life — don't let them get at you, don't let them trap you, don't let them squeeze you into the pit of conformity.

You are you. There is no one on earth like you. There never has been and never will be. Your views, approach, belief, prayers, thoughts, actions and life will be as no other. You are a gift to this world. A precious life.

Love yourself. Allow others to love you. Love others. Love life in all its incredible beauty.

31 A NEW WAY FORWARD

During these first years of ministry there have been many priests who have contacted me, fascinated by what I am doing. They have spoken to me of their frustration with the system and their sense of being prevented from being able to offer a proper priestly ministry. However, they have felt trapped. The transition from parish life to working independently is immense and too great for many to manage successfully, however much they may want to try.

I have written a number of times to various bishops, officials and the Archbishop of Canterbury hoping to establish some form of contact and communication. My experience and ministry, while happening outside the established church, is nevertheless available for all the Christian family.

Sadly, my overtures have all been ignored or rejected.

COMMITTEES FULL OF CANT, WITHOUT AN IDEA IN SIGHT

As the denominational churches thrash around for initiatives and projects to stimulate the faithful and halt the decline in church attendance, they set up endless committees.

The same people with the same ideas bore each other and the public into apathy and disdain. Cosmetic alterations are made, and artificial excitement is expressed at what are inconsequential changes.

There needs to be a massive shake up, a complete overhaul, a radically different approach.

UNWELCOME PROPHET

If you look down history, many changes in approach and attitude have come from unwelcome sources; and those pilloried in their time have often been respected later. Not that I want to boast that I am in that category. However, I sincerely believe that the true church of God, of which I am a priest and about which I care, can benefit and be refreshed by what I have begun.

I have no desire to damage the good and lovely work of God carried out across the nation. I only want to be a part of it, following the calling God has given me.

If those involved in the systems of religion today continue to view me with suspicion and threat, that will be their loss; I only hope and believe that in time a harvest of insights and opportunities flow from my ministry to the wider Christian family.

FOR GOD'S SAKE
DON'T GO TO CHURCH

There are some people, who would not be likely to grow beyond a certain point, who will find church life as it is today a safe haven and refuge. There are some people who may, through wise choices and through careful involvement, be able to achieve a position of independence and maturity within a church setting, but this is rare.

There is that host of others who maintain a superficial and thus safer relationship with a church, popping in now and then.

My book in part has been to warn that majority about the very real dangers of becoming closely involved in the local church as it is today.

This might be seen by the denominations to be negative. I would hope they could move beyond such a knee-jerk, defensive reaction and accept the invitation to change. Thus they could mature beyond the cosy cliques which most of the churches are today, and become the inclusive, accepting, forgiving and loving gathering of God's people, to which Jesus pointed. Such communities would be lifegiving and would pose no threat.

A CALL TO THE PRIESTS

Some priests are working unhappily in church settings, caught up in an endless round of diocesan and church business and meetings, pecked at daily by the same group of parishioners and hardly ever in contact with the majority of people in the area.

Is this what God called you to do?

There are others who for a variety of reasons have run into conflict with the powers that be and no longer have a parish. Yet you still believe in your priesthood and ministry and are grieved at the system's apparent ability to frustrate your calling.

Others have come unstuck at some point or other and may for many years have pursued other careers. However, whatever any officials may decide, you know that sufficient healing has taken place in your heart and soul to begin your priestly work again.

To all such priests there is the same challenge. Your life is the only life you will ever have. If you are not doing what you feel is right for your life and what you believe God wants you to be doing, then it is within your power to change that situation.

Don't wait to be given permission, or for doors to open. You have been given the responsibility and the commission by God to make your plans and your choices. No one else can do that for you. Don't waste the life, the priesthood and the ministry that is yours.

HELP AROUND THE
CORNER

I am very willing to advise priests and ministers on how they can go about setting up independently, and to speak with them about any other ideas they may have.

In the coming years, whether just a few or in many future decades, I am sure that a mobile, flexible and independent form of Christian ministry will inevitably emerge in this country.

When it does. let's hope it won't become institutionalised. There is that essential element, the heart of the faith, 'the spirit', likened by Jesus to the wind, which comes and goes, invisible, unpredictable, surprising and energising, leading us on, breaking down our preconceptions, challenging our neat and tidy lives and thoughts, keeping us on our toes, adventuring and exploring.

That spirit, 'the spirit of God', must never be lost from our lives. Once it is gone, we, or our organisation, are like a body after death, like a balloon deflated. The material is still there, but its essential life has drained away and rendered it useless.

THE LIVING BREATH

I once saw two frogs that had some time before been mating. One had died and the other had not stopped clinging to its decaying body. It was a disturbing sight.

Whether it be a religion, a church, a movement, a cause, a marriage, a relationship, whatever, once the spirit, the living breath has gone, decisions need to be taken for change.

In society and in the church there are so many of us who remain clinging to what is dead. Somehow owning the truth of what has happened, letting go and journeying anew is so terrifying that clinging to a corpse is preferable.

UNTOLD POSSIBILITIES

Yet there is so much to see, do, feel, know, experience and achieve. The universe is replete with mystery, the world and its continents with available adventures, our own land wide and vast. In addition, the realm of thought and imagination covers an even more tantalisingly infinite expanse. How tragic if some choice, religion or system should sentence you to eke out your days in a rut, in a soul-destroying situation, at a dead end.

Instead, allow for no such limitation. Realise how precious and important it is to preserve and protect the breath of life within you and your life as well as that spiritual flame which must burn for ever. If it should ever begin to fade or dim, do whatever it takes to maintain its light, its strength, its warmth and its hope; its vital supply of energy is love.

32

THE MOST AMAZING CATHEDRAL OF ALL – A SEWERAGE TANK

Some time ago I became involved in a very unusual project which resulted in my being appointed as the chairman of a newly formed charity called 'The Holy Circle Trust'.

The trust holds title to a piece of land off the London Road at Ryarsh near West Malling in Kent. The land had been used for a sewerage plant and it had become derelict and despoiled. Our vision of restoring the land and transforming it into a place of beauty and peace connected well with my own experiences and beliefs.

RESURRECTING A SHIT HOLE

The land had once cleansed our waste and provided pure fresh water for new life. Now this same land would welcome people wasted through life's struggle and renew and refresh them for their life's journey.

The place of human waste, pollution and contamination would become the fertile setting for creativity, for initiative and for hope. The very ground which knew the lowest would give birth to the highest.

The trust's plan was always to try to recreate what was there rather than assuming it should be removed or destroyed. Hence it was envisaged that the old sludge tank would become a place for meditation and peace, a haven from the pressures of life, a shelter for discovery and replenishment.

LOVE'S CATHEDRAL

At the heart of the land is one of the old sunken circular filtration tanks. It provides an extensive and remarkable open-air gathering space, roofed by the vast sky, surrounded by the sounds of nature and with natural amplification.

It represents a place of total safety and inviolability, where all can be in their own way, a sanctum for the world, a circle of love encompassing the variety of humankind.

SO IS THIS A CULT THING?

No way is this a new cult. We have been very careful to ensure, through its governing documents, that the trust can never represent any one person or group; nor can it be aligned to any organisation, faith or philosophy, or become a group in its own right.

The trust exists solely to provide a place of physical and spiritual refreshment for everyone, which belongs to everyone, which includes everyone and which welcomes everyone.

Those responsible for administering the trust do so because they wish to draw upon any resource from any origin which will enable them to create a place where unconditional love, welcome, acceptance, forgiveness, friendship, healing, respect, comfort, compassion, rest, solace, care, beauty, tranquillity, prayer, worship and peace can be experienced.

REFRESHMENT

Quiet walkways, sensitively planted gardens, running water, the occasional sheltered copse, orchards, meadow areas, grazing animals, a fish lake, vegetable and flower growing areas — the land will be a taste of paradise.

From the higher ground, visitors will have an overall perspective while moving through the land, which will allow them to be surprised by new sights and sounds and the fragrances of seasonal herbs and blooms.

Every one of us has different abilities, and care will be taken to ensure that the needs and enjoyment of all are fully considered.

DREAMS, VISIONS AND HOPE

The trust was formed and the landscape is being created because ordinary people were inspired to turn a dream into a reality. In a world which knows of such strife and misery caused by the difficulty we have in accepting and loving each other, the trust believes it important to provide the world with a symbol of the unity and peace which flows from love.

Here is a piece of land which is held in trust for every human being across the world. Here is a place from which no one is excluded and to which all are invited; where every person will enjoy the same position of respect, the same encouragement to be most fully human, the same affirmation to bless the land with their treasures and to be blessed by the treasures the land can yield.

Here is a tiny portion of the world which belongs to you and to every member of the wonderful human family.

LOVE'S INVITATION, LOVE'S GIFT

The land, though, is in the end just a symbol. What is important is not the land, not the symbol, but the reality to which the symbol points.

Love invites us to make of our lives and our circumstances the same all-inclusive, all-embracing, love-filled, restoring, renewing, and kindly experience symbolically expressed by the land.

As we live and grow and work within the real world love will come to us, constantly surprising us, empowering us, healing us and giving us the wings with which we can fly with freedom, become most fully ourselves, be able to delight in the wonder and the beauty of this world.

Wherever there is love there is life.

Love gives birth to love.

If you would be interested in supporting the work of the Holy Circle Trust and helping to realise its dream, please send a donation (made payable to 'The Holy Circle Trust') to:
Whispering Trees
273, Beechings Way
Gillingham
ME8 7BP
England
or phone 01634 262920 for further information
or pay it directly to the Trustee Savings Bank:
Sort Code 77–91–19
Account Number 90214160
Account Name: The Holy Circle Trust.